COCKTAILS ON TAP

TO MY PARENTS, WHO NEVER QUESTIONED TOO MUCH
MY DUBIOUS CAREER CHOICES

COCKTAILS ON TAP

THE ART OF MIXING SPIRITS AND BEER JACOB GRIER

FOREWORD BY STEPHEN BEAUMONT, PHOTOGRAPHS BY DAVID L. REAMER

STEWART, TABORI & CHANG, NEW YORK

CONTENTS

FOREWORD

WELCOME TO THE CURIOUS, SOMETIMES ODD, AND NEARLY ALWAYS INTERESTING WORLD OF BEER COCKTAILS. AS YOU'LL FIND IN THE FOLLOWING PAGES, RATHER THAN BEING A MERE AFFECTATION OF MODERN MIXOLOGY, DRINKS MADE WITH BEER AS AN INGREDIENT HAVE A LONG AND STORIED HISTORY, SPANNING CENTURIES AND CONTINENTS.

My personal history with beer cocktails, on the other hand, dates back a mere couple of decades, to when I "discovered" them in the altogether unlikely milieu of Paris, France.

The time was the mid- to late 1990s, and although I was by then an established beer scribe with a trio of books under my belt, family matters brought me to French wine country on a surprisingly regular basis, usually on visits ending with a few days in the capital. Thirsting for good beer after a week or two of wine drinking, I would prowl the handful of legitimate beer bars in Paris, eventually becoming fascinated by the lists of beer cocktails uniformly available in each and every one.

In retrospect, it all made much more sense than I then afforded it. Parisians are not by nature big beer drinkers, preferring instead to linger for as long as possible over a single diminutive glass of Kronenbourg 1664 or some similarly pallid and golden lager, usually on the terrace of a fine café. So in order to stimulate interest in their wares, Parisian beer bars would spice things up with a variety of mixes, from the ubiquitous Picon Bière, the story of which is found on page 43, to more inventive creations like the bière flambée, an entire 750-ml bottle of Chimay Première poured into an oversized chalice and topped with a generous, flaming floater of brandy.

My curiosity thus stimulated, I began to experiment with beer cocktails on my own, eventually establishing a small list of them in the Toronto beer cuisine restaurant and bar I helped open, beerbistro. Perhaps predictably, most were initially subject to, at best, extreme skepticism and, at worst, open derision, at least until the disbelievers allowed themselves a sip.

Time passes and minds open, however, and while it would be premature or even foolhardy to suggest that beer cocktails are today accepted without question, they are certainly less controversial and more commonly found than they were a decade or so ago. The book you now hold in your hands is testament to that fact, both in its existence and its contents.

What Jacob Grier and his merry band of collaborators have produced within the following pages puts my early and limited experimentations to shame. Following a suitably respectful look at hot and cold beer drinks of the distant and more recent past, Jake turns his considerable talents to expanding and, in some cases, redefining the lexicon of beer cocktails, a task he accomplishes with great style and taste. That his introductory notes for each drink make for such enjoyable, sometimes compelling, reading is just the proverbial icing on the cake—or in this case, I suppose, the garnish on the glass.

Beyond simply reading the recipes, of course you're going to want to mix a few, and in that regard I suggest beginning with a relatively simple one, perhaps my own creation on page 82, the Green Devil, which Jake kindly credits with inspiring his interest in beer cocktails. Once you've mastered such basics, try some that are a bit more involved, such as the quirky Kooey Kooey Kooey

(page 126), before dipping a toe into yesteryear with a vintage recipe from the first part of Chapter 1, like the wonderfully named Blow My Skull (page 39).

Thus introduced to the near-infinite flavors and aromas inherent in beer cocktails, it's my guess that it won't be long before you begin pulling out the pilsners and porters and IPAs and experimenting with your own formulations. And with the wealth of beers available today, what a long and fruitful journey that will be!

Stephen Beaumont, coauthor
of *The World Atlas of Beer*
and *The Pocket Beer Guide 2015*

Piña Pica (page 95)

REVIVING THE BEER COCKTAIL

ALTHOUGH THE UNITED STATES IS IN THE MIDST OF A CRAFT COCKTAIL RENAISSANCE THAT REVELS IN UNIQUE INGREDIENTS AND UNUSUAL COMBINATIONS, BEER REMAINS AN UNDERUTILIZED INGREDIENT BEHIND THE BAR.

A skeptical attitude toward mixing other ingredients with beer goes back a long time. "There's not much you can 'do' with beer, except indulge in the pleasant task of drinking it," says *Esquire's Handbook for Hosts* (1949). Until the last few years, that was the attitude in the craft cocktail world too.

Yet mixing with beer has a long and storied history, as even *Esquire's Handbook* attests. Despite the dismissive statement above, a number of drinks combining beer and other ingredients appear in the book, including classics like Mulled Ale, the Flip, and Lamb's Wool (pages 56, 63, and 72). Once staples of tavern life, by the mid-twentieth century these drinks had become relics of days gone by.

In the nineteenth century—and for hundreds of years before—using beer in drinks was absolutely normal. Adding sugar, spice, and spirits was common practice. So was heating beer over a fire or by plunging a red-hot poker into it, to serve it warm on a cold night.

Even the lines between food and drink were sometimes a bit blurry. Drinks like Aleberry, caudles, and possets were standard fare in homes and taverns. These combined beer or wine with grain, milk, cream, or eggs to thicken them, providing both nutrition and a warming drink.

Not all of these appeal to modern drinkers. "A terrible drink . . . with a terrible name," writes Alice Morse Earle in *Customs and Fashions in Old New England* (1894), was "whistle-belly vengeance. It consisted of sour household beer simmered in a kettle, sweetened with molasses, filled with brown-bread crumbs and drunk piping hot."

Historian Dorothy Hartley, in her 1954 book *Food in England*, explains that modern travelers, accustomed to comfortable transport and regular meals, no longer feel the need for such "soup wine" or "ale meal." When travel was harder and meals were scarce, these struck a happy medium for the weary traveler.

After long hours of travel, hot wine, or spirits, on an empty stomach, were not too good, and yet often you were too tired to eat. Thus, the compromise of a caudle, which warmed you, fed you, and "kept you going till you could obtain a solid meal."

Even in the 1950s, Hartley wrote that the custom of a "food drink" persisted among the working poor and rural folk. But by the latter half of the twentieth century, these drinks were well on their way out. What happened?

For one thing, the beer changed, and largely for the better. Owners of old-fashioned pubs and taverns didn't get their beer in sterile metal kegs or clean glass bottles like they do today. It was often brewed on site, a living thing kept at cellar temperatures in wooden casks and tended by the owner.

This sounds romantic—and good cask-conditioned ale today is rightfully held in high regard—but quality wasn't always assured. The ale could be too old, too yeasty, or spoiled by bacteria. It could be unpleasantly smoky with flavor carried over from barley malt roasted over flame. Or worse, it could have who-knows-what added to it to mask off flavors.

In his 1892 book *The Flowing Bowl*, William Schmidt cautioned drinkers about the adulterations common earlier in the century:

This healthy and agreeable beverage used to be prepared often enough from a mixture containing many violent poisons, as Indian hemp, opium, sulphuric acid, sulphate of iron, etc.—nay, the addition of strychnia, even was suspected.

The 1871 edition of *Oxford Night Caps* encourages readers to make drinks with home-brewed beer for the same reason, noting the various ways "common brewers and publicans" corrupted their beer with frightening additions. Presumably there was some exaggeration here, but if the beer was unreliable, one can imagine why drinkers liked to add sugar, spice, and everything nice to cover up its defects.

Technology changed all that. Railroads and mechanical refrigeration made it possible to transport beer over longer distances and keep it cold on the journey. Breweries grew larger, taking over the production of beer on regional and eventually national scales. Crisp, German-style lagers, served ice cold, replaced traditional English ales as the style of choice.

As the beer improved, the need to fix it up diminished. And even if patrons wanted the old-style beer drinks, the new lagers wouldn't have worked very well in them. A pint of mulled ale with spice and brandy is enticing; giving the same treatment to a lager isn't as appealing.

The bars changed too, with fancy cocktails individualized to suit the customer's taste replacing the communal punch bowl. The gallons of ale punch, wassail bowls, or refreshing "cups" of ale mixed with fruit, spirits, and spices gradually fell out of style as the age of cocktails took hold.

And, finally, a series of disastrous events in the early twentieth century took their toll on the alcohol business: two world wars, the Great Depression, and Prohibition. Breweries and distilleries shut down, and bartenders retired from the trade or moved to Europe. By the time things settled down, many of the old practices and ingredients had been forgotten. Cold beer and simple cocktails ruled the day.

Until recently, that is. The revival of American craft beer dates to the 1970s, with a community of homebrewers coming into its own, and Anchor Brewing and New Albion reviving the tradition of making quality ales. They set off a revolution in craft beer. Today, there are more than 2,500 breweries in the United States. Coupled with a strong import market, the quality and diversity of beers available here are without precedent.

The rebirth of cocktail and spirit culture took longer, in part because of stricter regulations on distillation; many brewers got their start making beer at home, but doing the same with spirits risks hefty fines and a prison sentence. Nonetheless, cocktail culture began reviving in earnest in the late 1990s, bringing back classic pre-Prohibition cocktails and driving interest in creative mixology using fresh fruits and herbs, obscure spirits, and inventive culinary techniques.

The market for spirits has expanded too, with imports like genever, Old Tom–style gin, mezcal, rhum agricole, cachaça, and Italian amaro enjoying renewed popularity. Smaller distilleries are following in the footsteps of beer brewers, rapidly expanding in number and creating new products with unusual ingredients.

Given the recent revivals of craft beer, quality spirits, and creative cocktails, it's no surprise that they are beginning to meet in the same glass. That this book took form in Portland, Oregon—one of the best cities in the world for brewing, distilling, and making cocktails—is not entirely surprising either.

Credit for spotting this trend before it developed goes to my friend Ezra Johnson-Greenough, a Portland-based beer blogger, event organizer, and label artist for several local breweries. Seeing the potential for mixing spirits and beer, he came up with the idea for Brewing Up Cocktails, an event featuring an entire menu of cocktails using beer as an ingredient. He recruited me and Yetta Vorobik, owner of the Hop and Vine bar in Portland, to help make it happen.

The event successfully bridged the gap between Portland's beer and cocktail communities and became the first of many of our collaborations. Over the next four years, we held Brewing Up Cocktails events in Portland, Seattle, Vancouver, San Francisco, and New Orleans. These were often built around themes, such as tropical cocktails or drinks made with eggs, or around the portfolio of beers from an individual brewery.

As our experience grew, so did our sense of how to use beer as an ingredient. It can be tricky, and in our early days we tried some experiments that are better left forgotten. But through trial and error, research, and the eager consumption of beer cocktails invented by our colleagues in the bar industry, we came to develop an understanding of the great variety of ways beer can be used in mixed drinks.

As the pages that follow will demonstrate, beer can be used as a wonderfully versatile ingredient in cocktails. Various styles of beer can stimulate all of our basic senses of taste. Dark roasted malts and aggressive hops can add bitterness to a drink. Sour ales like Berliner weisse and lambic can provide acidity. Fruity beer or rich, malty ale can sweeten a cocktail. Even salt and umami can sometimes be found in beer, with the former an ingredient in German *gose* and adventurous brewers trying out such ingredients as seaweed and bacon. The carbonation in beer can also serve to lighten and lengthen a drink, providing an interesting alternative to sodas and sparkling wine. With beer offering so many different possibilities for cocktails, able to suit all palates and occasions, I felt compelled to spread the word.

This book is a distillation of six years of experience drinking beer cocktails and creating them for bar menus and special events. Chapter 1 digs into old books for the beer cocktails of the past, whether they be straightforward punches or easy ways of spicing up a basic lager. Chapter 2 looks at the lost art of serving beer hot, from simple mulled ales to strange yet tasty concoctions unlike anything found in (most) bars today. Finally, Chapter 3 takes up contemporary mixology in all its glorious creativity, working modern beer styles, varied spirits, and house-made ingredients into deliciously unique cocktails.

When I first got into beer cocktails, they were few and far between on most cocktail menus. Writing this book, I encountered so many that I couldn't possibly include them all. I've done my best to narrow them down so as to showcase as wide a variety of ingredients and techniques as possible. I hope that it will continue to inspire the mingling of beers and spirits, bringing beer back to a deservedly prominent place in the bartender's arsenal.

SEVEN STYLES OF BEER COCKTAILS

LIKE BEER ITSELF, BEER COCKTAILS COME IN SO MANY VARIETIES THAT ANY ATTEMPT TO MAKE FIRM CLASSIFICATIONS AMONG THEM IS BOUND TO LEAVE A FEW THINGS OUT. NONETHELESS, THERE ARE A FEW TYPES OF BEER COCKTAILS THAT COME UP REPEATEDLY, PATTERNS IN MIXING THAT CAN BE USED AS TEMPLATES TO CREATE NEW DRINKS.

PREPARED BEERS

The simplest beer cocktails, these are beers that are modified with spirits, spices, or other ingredients to take on additional flavor. The Boilermaker (whiskey dropped into a pint of beer, page 42) is an obvious example. The Michelada (beer accented with citrus and seasonings, page 41) and the Picon Bière (beer with bitter orange liqueur, page 43) are other classics in the style. Beer remains the main ingredient in these drinks and they're generally served in a large glass.

BEER-TOPPED COCKTAILS

These are drinks in which the base could almost stand as a cocktail by itself, combining spirits, juices, and syrups, often shaken or stirred with ice before being poured into the serving glass. A complementary beer is then poured on top of this mixture, much as one might pour soda or ginger ale into a long drink. Many contemporary beer cocktails, like the Dark and Stoutly (page 140) or the Portland Rickey (page 133), take this approach.

BEER-INCORPORATED COCKTAILS

These are drinks in which beer is treated just like any other ingredient, shaken or stirred along with everything else. This approach works especially well in tiki cocktails, where shaking a bitter beer such as an IPA with the rum, juice, and syrups gives a touch of bitterness and a big, frothy head. The Mai Ta-IPA (page 91), Iron Island (page 130), and a few other entries in Chapter 3 use this technique.

BEER FLIPS

Modern "flip" cocktails are made using a whole egg. Early recipes for flips involved heating rum and beer with a hot poker, with or without eggs. Contemporary flips tend to be shaken with ice and served cold. Regardless, the use of dark beer in egg drinks is a winning combination, and it turns up in the Averna Stout Flip (page 149) and Beer Nog (page 116).

COCKTAILS WITH BEER SYRUPS

Sometimes the use of beer in a cocktail starts long before serving the drink. Beer can be reduced on the stove and combined with sugar and spices to make a flavorful syrup. Fruity lambics are prime candidates for this treatment, although dark beers can work too, as demonstrated in the Vandaag Gin Cocktail (page 111) and the Bolt Cutter (page 142). Beer can even be cooked into a jam, as in the Ramble On (page 109).

BEER PUNCHES

Beer has a long history in punch, to which it both adds its own flavor and balances the strength of higher-proof spirits. The Ale Punch (page 33), Brown Betty (page 38), Blow My Skull (page 39), and Abbey Street Punch (page 124) are all excellent examples of punches that call for beer. Though most of the recipes in this book are scaled for the indi-vidual cocktail, these are wonderful for entertaining larger groups. A bowl of beer punch relieves the host of bartender duty and provides a convivial spot for guests to gather.

HOT BEER DRINKS

Hot beer drinks may sound strange, but they were once an important part of drinking culture. On a cold night, they can be just the thing to shake off a chill. I've devoted an entire chapter to these drinks in the hope of reviving them for a modern audience that has likely never had the pleasure of tasting them (see pages 52–79).

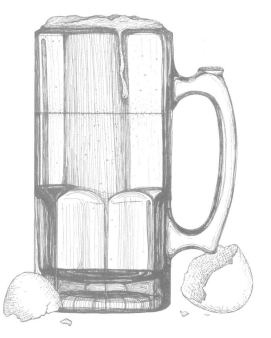

MIXING 101

THE DRINKS IN THIS BOOK ARE MADE WITH STANDARD COCKTAIL TECHNIQUES AND TOOLS, MANY OF WHICH ARE LIKELY ALREADY IN YOUR HOME BAR OR KITCHEN. IF NOT, THEY CAN ALL BE PICKED UP FAIRLY AFFORDABLY. HERE, I COVER COCKTAIL TOOLS AND BASIC TECHNIQUES THAT WILL COME IN HANDY FOR THE DRINKS AHEAD. THEY'RE NOT ALL ESSENTIAL, BUT HAVING THE RIGHT TOOLS ON HAND MAKES ANY JOB EASIER, AND A WELL-MADE PIECE OF KIT MAKES DOING A JOB MORE ENJOYABLE.

TOOLS

JIGGER

Precision is important when making cocktails. Spirits are strong ingredients and using just a tad too much or too little of them can throw off the balance of a drink. Exact measures ensure quality and consistency.

Professional bartenders tend to use two-ended metal jiggers of different sizes, each measuring a different volume. These are great for a high-speed bar environment, but for home use I usually reach for something simpler. The kitchen equipment brand Oxo makes mini angled measuring cups that are nearly perfect for making cocktails, with measurements marked from 1/4 ounce to 2 ounces (60 ml); these

are what I find most convenient for casual drink-making at home. In a bar or other professional setting, I prefer the ProJig from Über Bar Tools, which divides the traditional jigger into multiple compartments.

living serving drinks. For stirred cocktails, there are plenty of attractive glass and crystal options on the market, but many vessels could work. At home, I have been using the bottom half of a glass French-press coffee maker, because I am writing full-time and cannot afford nicer things.

BAR SPOON

A long-handled spoon is useful for stirring drinks and occasionally for measuring ingredients that can tolerate some imprecision. I find that spoons with a tight spiral or no spiral at all are most comfortable to use and are easiest to twirl between one's fingers. This is one item that I believe is worth spending some money on, as being able to deftly stir a cocktail looks cool and feels great. Standard kitchen spoons do not lend themselves to the rapid, smooth stirring ideal for chilling and diluting a cocktail.

COCKTAIL STRAINER

You will likely encounter two types of cocktail strainers: Hawthorne

SHAKER/MIXING GLASS

The most versatile tool for mixing drinks is a Boston shaker, a combination of pint glass and metal tin (cup). Shaken drinks are built in the glass, the metal tin is secured firmly over the top of it, and then all is shaken. Three-piece cobbler shakers (pictured on page 19) are also popular. Stirred drinks can be built directly into the glass and stirred with a long-handled spoon.

My preference is to use separate tools for shaken and stirred drinks, choosing ones ideally suited to each task. This maximizes efficiency behind the bar; for casual home use, it's more of a stylistic choice. I use a large metal tin and small "cheater" tin for shaken cocktails, which is lighter than glass—an important consideration if you make your and julep. Hawthorne strainers are the kind with a metal coil wrapped around them. Julep strainers are made of concave, perforated metal. Traditionally, Hawthornes are used for shaken drinks, juleps for stirred. Are both necessary? Not really. A Hawthorne handles both duties just fine.

SMALL FINE-MESH STRAINER

One item that definitely should not be overlooked is a small fine-mesh strainer, also known as a tea strainer. This is used in addition to a Hawthorne strainer to catch shards of ice and bits of herbs or other ingredients and keep them out of the finished drink. Without it, shaken cocktails will come out with a crunchy surface.

LARGE FINE-MESH STRAINER

A few drinks or syrups require straining larger quantities of liquid, for which a large strainer comes in handy.

JUICER

You could make cocktails with store-bought citrus juice from a bottle. You could also buy a Bud Light Beer-ita cocktail in a can. I can't recommend either course of action. Squeeze fresh juice for cocktails to achieve the best results. A small handheld citrus squeezer is good for lemons and limes, and a larger handheld squeezer or manual reamer is good for grapefruits and oranges.

MICROPLANE OR SPICE GRATER

Similarly, freshly grated spices are much more aromatic than ground spices from a jar. A Microplane is useful for freshly grating spices, especially nutmeg

and cinnamon, which are often called for to garnish the surface of cocktails and punches.

GLASS BOTTLES AND JARS

Some of the drinks in this book call for homemade syrups or other ingredients, so having a few empty bottles and jars in which to store them is helpful.

BLENDER

Though there are no blended drinks in this book, a blender is needed for making a couple of the homemade cocktail ingredients. A handheld immersion blender is convenient for these and is a useful culinary tool.

ICE MOLDS

In recent years, bartenders have become obsessed with fancy ice. This is, on the whole, a good thing,

as a lot of the ice out there is small, wet, and airy, and will melt rapidly into drinks and water them down. Some bars go to extraordinary lengths to get the hardest, clearest ice they can find, up to buying sculpture-quality blocks and breaking them down with chainsaws.

This is a bit much for the home bartender. It is nice to have good ice on hand, though—ice that is regularly shaped, hard throughout, and relatively free of the air that many icemakers introduce. Silicone molds for small, large, and very large cubes are available, and I recommend them. There are also a few molds on the market for making spheres, if you want to get fancy. A small bowl or pan is also useful for freezing blocks of ice for punches.

MUDDLER

A muddler is a long, blunt tool used for crushing ingredients in the bottom of a glass or shaker (or for evicting unruly patrons). It's usually made of metal or wood. My favorite is the handmade PUG! wooden muddler, available online. It fits my hand better than any other I have tried.

POTS

The hot drinks in the book will need to be prepared on the stove. A small pot is good for individual-size drinks, and a larger pot can be used for drinks made in larger batches. These will also be useful for the homemade syrups called for in some recipes.

THERMOMETER

A thermometer isn't in the usual bartender's toolbox, but it comes in handy for the chapter on hot drinks. One could make these drinks by feel, but a candy or deep-fry thermometer is more reliable.

GLASSWARE

Many of the drinks in this book can be served in typical barware: a tall collins or highball glass, a cocktail or martini glass, and a rocks glass. A few call for shot glasses. Beer glasses, such as a pint glass, German beer stein, and a chalice or flute, are also used in some recipes. Hot drinks should be served in ceramic or tempered-glass mugs.

MEASURING CUP

A liquid measuring cup (usually glass, with a spout for pouring) is necessary for measuring ingredients when making punches or homemade ingredients.

MEASURING

Jiggers only provide accurate measures when they're used correctly. For a traditional metal jigger, this means making sure it is held level and filling it completely until a meniscus forms at the top. For nontraditional jiggers, make sure they are held level and that liquids meet measurement lines precisely.

BUILDING A DRINK

When preparing the ingredients for a cocktail, pour them in the order given. If building them in a mixing glass or shaker, pour the liquids in before adding ice, so that the ice doesn't melt while the ingredients are being added.

STIRRING

Stirring chills ingredients without aerating them. Generally, drinks that do not use juices, eggs, or cream can be stirred instead of shaken. Use a long spoon to smoothly turn ice through the liquid until the drink is thoroughly chilled. This takes longer than shaking and depends significantly on the ice being used, but a good target is 30 to 45 seconds. Let taste be your guide.

DRY SHAKING

A "dry shake" is when the ingredients are shaken without ice. This is done to aerate them and make them frothy. Bartenders use this technique most often with egg whites.

SHAKING

Combine all the ingredients with ice and firmly seal the shaker. With one hand on each end of the shaker, shake until the ingredients are thoroughly chilled. This is a fast process, generally the work of 5 to 10 seconds. Shake rapidly and hard! As one of my mentors put it, "You're waking the cocktail up, not putting it to sleep."

STRAINING

Straining separates the cocktail from the ice used to chill it, so that it can be poured over fresh ice or served without it. Generally speaking, it's best to strain a cocktail into a chilled glass to keep the drink cold.

A julep strainer or Hawthorne strainer can be used for stirred drinks. For shaken drinks, it's best to use a Hawthorne and a fine-mesh strainer together, "double straining" the cocktail by placing the second strainer between the shaker and the glass. This removes any ice shards or fragments of other ingredients that pass through the Hawthorne.

HEATING

The drinks in Chapter 2 are served hot. Heating beer accentuates its bitterness, so it's important to heat it gradually and evenly. Place beer and any other ingredients called for in a pot over low to medium heat and clip a thermometer to the pot. Heat the beer to the temperature indicated by the recipe—I find that 140°F (60°C) is a good target temperature for serving hot beer drinks. Serve it much cooler and the drink will become tepid; much hotter and the drink will be too bitter. Pour hot drinks

into warmed mugs to maintain the target drink temperature.

GARNISHING

Some garnishes just look pretty or provide a tasty snack for the drinker. Others, such as spices, herbs, or citrus, provide aromatics too. Use the right techniques to get the most out of aromatic garnishes: Grate spices freshly and lightly smack leafy herbs to release their aromas. Many of the following recipes call for twists of citrus as garnish, and you should make the most of the flavorful oils that they can add to a cocktail. Take a thin swath of peel and twist or pinch it over the glass, peel side down, to "express" the citrus oil onto the surface of the drink.

STERILIZING

Some recipes require making syrups and jams, which can be stored and used long after that first cocktail, but you need to make sure your storage containers are clean. To sterilize a bottle or mason jar, wash it thoroughly in hot soapy water and rinse. Put it right side up in a pot along with the lid and the ends of the tongs. Completely cover them with water then boil over high heat for 15 minutes. Use the tongs to remove the jar. Pour out the water, and while the jar is still hot, fill it with warm ingredients. (Adding hot ingredients to a cool jar may cause the jar to crack.) Use the tongs to remove the lid, then seal the jar.

EGG SAFETY

Several of the drinks in this book are mixed with raw eggs. Although the risk of illness is remote, it is possible to transmit salmonella via uncooked eggs. Keeping eggs refrigerated and taking care to handle them cleanly will minimize this risk. Those with compromised immune systems may wish avoid these drinks.

BEER AND SPIRIT STYLES

WHENEVER POSSIBLE IN THE RECIPES THAT FOLLOW, I'VE AVOIDED CALLING FOR SPECIFIC BRANDS. I WANT THIS BOOK TO BE APPROACHABLE AND FOR THE DRINKS TO BE MADE AND ENJOYED BY READERS. SO WITH THAT IN MIND, THE RECIPES TEND TO IDENTIFY INGREDIENTS BY GENERAL STYLE.

A cocktail recipe might call for "gin" or "IPA," but the brand to use is up to you. For many spirit and beer styles, there are so many good examples on the market that for me to call any out for particular use would be completely arbitrary.

That doesn't mean one should just reach for the cheap stuff. Better ingredients do make a better cocktail. But there's no need to go overboard with expensive ingredients or stress out about picking exactly the right bourbon or lager to put into a drink. Choose something good and moderately priced; if there's a brand you particularly like to drink on its own, it will probably do nicely in a cocktail too.

Information on some of the more esoteric ingredients is given in the individual drink descriptions. When a cocktail's creator prefers one brand, that's included too.

The one big exception to all of this is the chapter on hot drinks. For these, you really do have to try to get as close as possible to the old, malty style of English ales that were available at the time of these drinks' original popularity. Contemporary American takes on malty ales, even ones that are nominally English in style, often tend to balance the maltiness with healthy doses of hops. These taste great cold, but when served hot, that hoppy bitterness can throw a drink out of balance. See the introduction to that chapter (page 55) for more information on choosing the right ale for warm drinks.

A NOTE ON SOUS VIDE

The recipes in Chapter 2 have all been written with instructions for making drinks on a standard stovetop. However, there is another option for heating beer cocktails: preparing them sous vide.

In sous-vide cooking, food is vacuum-sealed in a plastic bag and placed in a hot water bath, the temperature of which is controlled by a circulator. The food warms gradually and does not overcook since it cannot get hotter than the water surrounding it. So, for example, a chef can use sous-vide preparation to bring a steak to a perfect medium-rare, then give it a quick sear before serving it. It's a precise and forgiving way of cooking.

For the same reason, sous-vide is great for making warm beer cocktails. It allows them to heat gradually and ensures that they do not get too hot. And since the bag is a sealed environment, there is no risk of evaporation. The beer, spices, and other ingredients can be held together at a warm temperature for a longer time, extracting more flavor.

I teamed up with Chef Anthony Cafiero of the modernist restaurant Ración in Portland to try several of the drinks in this chapter as sous-vide preparations. They came out wonderfully, served at the perfect temperature and with no unpleasant bitterness.

Sous vide has mostly been the realm of the professional chef, but it is gradually making its way into home kitchens. To prepare beer cocktails sous vide, one needs an immersion circulator, a vacuum sealer, and sealable plastic bags. Good circulators can now be bought for less than $200. Not all vacuum sealers are designed to handle liquids, but ones that do are beginning to fall in price as well, although they are still expensive.

Mulled Ale (page 56), Dog's Nose (page 59), and Hot Bruin (page 79) are prime candidates for preparing sous vide. To make them, simply combine all the ingredients in a bag and seal them under a vacuum. Place them in a hot water bath set to 140°F (60°C) and let them sit for 45 minutes to 1 hour. Remove from the bath, cut the bag open, and pour the warm drink into a heated mug.

A NOTE ON AUTHENTICITY

Most of the first half of this book is dedicated to recipes for vintage drinks, often dating back centuries. Re-creating these drinks exactly isn't always possible because the ingredients themselves have changed, mostly for the better. Beer is of a more consistent quality, more reliably bubbly, and much less likely to be spoiled. It has also tended to become less malty and somewhat hoppier, at least where ales are concerned.

Spirits have also changed. Once sold at high proof by the barrel, in the United States they now tend to come at a standard of around 80 proof in glass bottles. The barrel aging is done in advance. Sugar, too, is different from what it once was. It's purer and more refined. Sugar loaves of the 1800s were hard enough to use for grating lemon zest, but good luck trying that today.

All things considered, there is no better time to be a connoisseur of alcoholic drinks. The quality and variety of beers and spirits available today is better than at any time before. But with the advances in making beers and spirits, re-creating the recipes of the past requires a bit of approximation and adaptation.

When necessary, I've adapted the drinks to fit modern measurements, ingredients, garnishes, and palates. Sometimes that's as simple as reducing the volumes of the recipes, with the days of tavern patrons downing a gallon of flip per sitting thankfully in the past. At other times, it means being selective about the beers used, or adding a bit more sugar to compensate for today's fully fermented ales. Whenever there is a significant departure, I note the change and reference the source of the original for anyone who desires to look it up.

These recipes are not always "authentic" in the sense of being exact replicas of the past, as that is not always practical. But they do attempt to capture what made those recipes appealing. This book will, I hope, bring some forgotten beverages back to life.

Beer cocktails are often treated like a modern trend, but the idea of mixing with beer is pretty much as old as beer itself.

Since long before (and after) the *Reinheitsgebot*—the famous German "beer purity law" of the fifteenth century that restricted lager brewers to using only barley, hops, water, and eventually yeast—people have made beer with all sorts of stuff.

Many historic ale and beer recipes would have never passed muster under Reinheitsgebot. The earliest Egyptian beers were so thick with grains and herbs that they had to be consumed through a straw. In more recent centuries, oats or rye meal often stood in for barley.

Brewers by necessity regularly supplemented grains with other forms of fermentable sugar, often molasses. Herbs and spices like sage, spruce, and cloves were used for flavor. Bicarbonate of soda could be added to stale beer to liven it up with carbonation. Or consider Cock Ale, a recipe from 1780, that called for the blood of an old rooster: "Slay, caw, and gut him, and stamp in a stone mortar. Add spice and put all in a canvas bag. Lower him into the ale while still working. Finish working and bottle." Contemporary beers brewed with sea urchins, bull testicles, or doughnuts (to name three recent examples from American brewers) don't seem that crazy by comparison.

Early American colonists drank ale, cider, and spirits in abundance. Even the children were in on it. An eighteenth-century almanac advised feeding kids a meal of brown bread, cheese, and warm beer. And if a child was sick, they could be cured with a dose of "admirable and most famous Snail water," a cure that sounds more frightening than most diseases. Garden snails were washed in beer, baked in an oven, and crushed in a mortar. To these crushed dried snails were added 1 quart of sliced earthworms; a variety of herbs, roots, and flowers; and then finally 3 gallons of strong ale. After sitting overnight, 2 spoonfuls of this concoction mixed with 4 spoonfuls of beer would be fed to the ailing child. It was certainly an incentive to get better.

Though I tried many unusual recipes while researching this book, I'll confess that I let the snail water pass without a taste test. Adventurous readers can look up the recipe in Alice Morse Earle's *Customs and Fashions in Old New England* and let me know if I'm missing out.

The point is, drinks that combine beer and other ingredients go back centuries. Though they wouldn't have been called "cocktails" then—that word was reserved specifically for drinks made with spirits, sugar, water, and bitters—these drinks certainly fit our looser modern definition of the word.

These beverages tended to be simpler than what one might find on a fancy modern cocktail menu. They combined locally popular beer styles with other available ingredients, such as a shandy containing ale and ginger beer or a punch containing porter and rum. Other drinks used liqueurs, spices, or citrus to add flavor to straightforward lagers.

Many of the recipes that follow call for English-style ales. For a few suggestions for beers that work particularly well in these vintage recipes, see page 55.

Some of the drinks in this chapter are likely familiar and continue to be served today. Others are largely forgotten and deserving of revival. All of them belie their simplicity with a finely tuned balance of flavors.

Our exploration of vintage beer cocktails starts with a Bang. This drink is recorded in Robert Kemp Philp's 1860 book *The Practical Housewife*. It's a simple combination of the alcoholic beverages Americans would have had in abundance in the 1800s. Here's the original recipe:

Take a pint of cider, and add to a pint of warm ale; sweeten with treacle or sugar to taste, grate in some nutmeg and ginger, and add a wine-glassful of gin or whiskey.

Refrigeration is cheaper now than it was in the 1800s, so I'd suggest ignoring the instruction to serve it warm and omitting the sugar. A mild English-style ale and a dry cider, both well chilled, work perfectly here. The gin from this period would likely mean genever, the malty, whiskeylike ancestor of gin imported from Holland. For the whiskey, I would choose a good, mid-priced bourbon. Though not traditional, a quality aged rum with some character could also be used.

The Bang is similar to the modern Snakebite, a 50/50 mix of cider and beer. That's a fine drink, but adding whiskey or genever and a little bit of spice gives it greater depth. If you double the recipe below, a standard American 12-ounce bottle each of cider and beer will make enough for two without any going to waste.

1 oz. whiskey or genever

Pinch of freshly grated nutmeg

Approximately 1/2 tsp. grated peeled fresh ginger

6 oz. (180 ml) ale

6 oz. (180 ml) cider

Pour the whiskey or genever into a large beer glass, grate in the nutmeg, and add the ginger. Top with the ale and cider, stir gently to combine, and serve.

Serves 1

If asked to nominate the most influential bartender of all time, many mixologists today would no doubt choose Jerry Thomas. Thomas traveled the world and worked his way up to becoming America's first celebrity bartender, holding court at the best bars in New York and San Francisco during the golden age of cocktails in the mid-1800s.

He accomplished much more than that, though. When his book, *Bar-Tender's Guide*, was published in 1862, he achieved something that no one before had attempted: He took the arcane knowledge of how to mix drinks, passed down from professional to professional, and presented it in an organized, accessible format. He classified the great variety of drinks that had become fashionable by their common elements in sensible categories: juleps, fizzes, collinses, cocktails, punches, and more. Thomas's book became an essential guide and has been published in various editions and plagiarized for decades.

Beer appears in only a few of the recipes in *Bar-Tender's Guide*, including the Ale Sangaree (page 34), the Flip (page 63), and this Ale Punch that uses a mild, English-style ale as the main ingredient; the readily available Old Speckled Hen is an excellent and affordable choice. The punch is easy to make, refreshing, and perfect for a party when you don't want to be stuck mixing individual cocktails.

The one tricky ingredient is capillaire. This originated as an allegedly medicinal infusion of maidenhair fern, a syrup I've only once come across for sale commercially (look for *xarope de capile* if you happen to be in Portugal). It evolved into a rich sugar syrup subtly characterized by an orange aroma. It may not have many curative qualities this way, but it's a tasty addition to punch and saves the trouble of tracking down good maidenhair fern.

ALE PUNCH

1 qt. (960 ml) ale

2 oz. (60 ml) fresh lemon juice

2 oz. (60 ml) Capillaire, *see recipe below*

2 oz. (60 ml) brandy

2 oz. (60 ml) dry white wine

Peel of 1 lemon, cut into wide swaths

Freshly grated nutmeg, for garnish

Combine all the ingredients in a punch bowl, finishing with a generous grating of nutmeg. Slip a large ice block into the bowl and ladle the punch into tumblers or punch glasses, or serve it over large ice cubes in individual glasses.

Serves 6 to 8

CAPILLAIRE*
*Adapted from a recipe by David Wondrich

2 cups (400 g) sugar

1 cup (240 ml) water

1/8 tsp. orange flower water

Combine the sugar and water in a pot over medium heat and stir until the sugar has dissolved. Stir in the orange flower water, transfer the syrup to a bottle, seal, and refrigerate. It should keep for several weeks.

Makes about 2 cups (480 ml)

Nowadays, if a patron walks into a brewpub and asks to have sugar and nutmeg added to his beer, he may receive a dubious glare from the brewmaster. But a couple of centuries ago, these ingredients formed a very popular beverage known as the Ale Sangaree.

Sangaree, like contemporary *sangria*, derives from *sangre*, Spanish for "blood." Cocktail historian Ted "Dr. Cocktail" Haigh traces the drink's roots to Spain and the Antilles islands (to their brothels, specifically), where it began life as a single serving of punch made with Indonesian arrack, a rumlike spirit distilled from sugar cane and red rice. By the 1800s, the drink had adopted multiple guises combining various alcoholic ingredients with sugar and nutmeg, with fortified wine from Madeira being one of the most popular. Jerry Thomas's definitive *Bar-Tender's Guide* included six different versions of sangaree, made with port, sherry, brandy, gin, ale, and porter.

The Port Wine Sangaree was the most popular of these in Thomas's day, though even by then the drink was on the wane. The ale version merits attention too. Though not the most complicated of drinks, its simplicity is pleasing. Choose a mild English or Scottish ale and a sugar with some character, such as Demerara or turbinado. To make a Porter Sangaree or "Porteree," follow the procedure below but substitute porter for ale.

ALE SANGAREE

1 tsp. sugar

12 to 16 oz. (360 to 480 ml) mild ale

Freshly grated nutmeg, for garnish

In a beer glass, dissolve the sugar in a splash of ale or water, muddling it, if necessary, to help it along. Top it with the ale and grate a little nutmeg over the surface of the drink.

Serves 1

SHANDYGAFF

1 oz. orange brandy liqueur, such as Grand Marnier

3/4 oz. fresh lemon juice

10 oz. (300 ml) English-style ale

10 oz. (300 ml) ginger beer

Twist of lemon peel, for garnish

Pour the liqueur and lemon juice into your "favourite tankard" (as Mr. Dickens recommends) along with a few large chunks of ice, then top with the ale and ginger beer. Stir gently to combine. Garnish with the lemon peel.

Serves 1

Though this book is mostly dedicated to mixing beer with spirits, some of the world's most popular beer drinks are created by mixing beer with non-alcoholic ingredients. The best known of these are Germany's *radler*, England's shandy, and France's *panaché*, all made by mixing light, effervescent beers in approximately equal volume with ginger beer or sparkling lemonade. These drinks are tasty and refreshing, and have the added virtue of being "sessionable"— meaning one can enjoy a few of them without being overcome by the effects of alcohol.

The origins of the shandy are lost to history, though it was known well enough to be referenced in *The Adventures of Mr. Verdant Green*, an 1853 novel about a freshman at Oxford. Mr. Green states in the book that a friend taught him "to make shandygaff and sherry-cobbler, and brew bishop and egg flip: oh, it's capital!"

The etymology of the shandygaff is equally mysterious, though Evan Morris speculates in his syndicated Word Detective column that it may derive from a combination of words basically meaning "loud nonsense." It certainly fits the image of someone who's had a few too many of the drinks, but no one knows for sure.

What we do know is that it's a very tasty drink. The variation here is adapted from a recipe in *Drinking with Dickens*, a wonderful book by Charles Dickens's great-grandson Cedric about old English drinking culture. The addition of orange liqueur makes this a little less sessionable, but I like the flavor it contributes.

BROWN BETTY

⅓ cup (75 g) packed brown sugar

1 cup (240 ml) water

½ lemon, sliced into wheels

16 oz. (480 ml) English-style ale

4 oz. (120 ml) brandy

Pinch of ground cloves

Pinch of ground cinnamon

In a bowl, dissolve the brown sugar in the water. Add the lemon slices and let them infuse for 15 minutes. Add the remaining ingredients, stir well, and serve over large ice cubes in tumblers or punch glasses.

Serves 4

Oxford University's guide to "famous Oxonians" boasts 26 prime ministers, 50 Nobel Prize winners, 12 saints, and 120 Olympic medalists.

The long list stretches from Stephen Hawking in the present day to William Ockham in the fourteenth century.

Mysteriously absent from the list is Richard Cook, to whom we owe a debt of gratitude for preserving one of the university's most important contributions to culture: the impressive variety of recipes its students relied upon to get drunk.

Cook published the first edition of his *Oxford Night Caps* in 1835. The 1871 edition has been recently reprinted, and it's a treasure trove of historic drinks and drinking traditions.

Take the Oxford Grace Cup, for example. This was a combination of beer and wine made in a vessel large enough for an entire party to sip from. The first imbiber would make a toast "to Church and King" while the guests at his right and left stood by his side. The Grace Cup would then make its way around the table, each person sipping from it while the two at his sides stood watch.

The practice was said to derive from when England was invaded by the Danes, "who frequently used to stab or cut the throats of the natives while they were drinking, the persons standing being the sureties that the one holding the cup should come to no harm while partaking of it."

Hopefully one's own guests can be trusted to refrain from violence. If entertaining a group, I recommend making another of the drinks recorded in Cook's collection, the Brown Betty, "said to have derived its name from one of the fair sex."

Cook writes that it is good either hot or cold, though I lean toward the latter. Use a good English ale, such as Samuel Smith's Winter Welcome or Abbot Ale.

As I began researching this book, one of the people I reached out to for inspiration was drink historian David Wondrich, author of the indispensable books *Imbibe!* and *Punch*. I knew that if anyone could alert me to some esoteric recipe that I'd overlooked, David would be the one. I asked him if anything came to mind, and he directed me right away to this corker. It has bold flavors from high-proof Jamaican pot-still rum, smoothed out nicely by the deft use of dark porter.

This drink comes from *The English and Australian Cookery Book: Cookery for the Many, As Well as the Upper Ten Thousand.* Published in 1864 by Edward Abbott, a member of the Tasmanian Parliament, it is considered Australia's first cookbook. In addition to standard English fare, it includes local delicacies such as roast wombat and "slippery bob," a dish comprised of kangaroo brains fried in emu fat. We'll stick to the drinks.

Abbott's drink chapter covers much of the same ground as other English-language drink books of the day, but one entry that stands out as unique is the aptly named Blow My Skull. According to Abbott, this was the favorite drink of an eccentric Tasmanian governor who possessed "a stronger head than most of his subordinates." The governor hosted banquets at which he would serve barbecued pig and a cask of this punch. Attendees feared being challenged to go drink for drink with him:

BLOW MY SKULL

3/4 cup (130 g) coarse sugar, preferably Demerara

1 qt. (960 ml) boiling water

16 oz. (480 ml) Jamaican pot-still rum

16 oz. (480 ml) porter

8 oz. (240 ml) brandy

6 oz. (180 ml) fresh lime juice

In a large bowl, dissolve the sugar in the boiling water. Add the remaining ingredients, stir, and refrigerate for several hours. When ready to serve, slip a large block of ice into the bowl. (If a block of ice is unavailable, add ice to cups individually.) Ladle the punch into cups to serve.

Serves 6

"No heel taps!" called out the governor in a voice of authority, and the unfortunate stranger was at once hors de combat; *while the governor having an impenetrable cranium, and an iron frame, could take several goblets of the alcoholic fluid, and walk away as lithe and happy as possible, attended by an orderly who could scarcely preserve his equilibrium.*

"Heel taps," by the way, is slang for a small amount of liquor left in glasses after drinking.

A drink with this reputation deserves a big, burly rum like Smith & Cross from Jamaica; for the brandy, use something cheap and strong.

I fondly remember my first experience drinking a Michelada, if not so much the night that came before it. I was on a trip to Tequila, Mexico, with a group of West Coast bartenders. We had an overnight flight on Halloween taking us from San Francisco to Guadalajara, and so the evening leading up to departure was spent enjoying San Francisco cocktail bars in our costumes. Then we managed to pour through two bottles of tequila and one of Fernet-Branca just on the short bus ride to the airport. It's a miracle we all managed to board the plane—and, indeed, one of us didn't.

When we arrived in Mexico the next morning, dressed like superheroes and hungover like mere mortals, we promptly sought out the hair of the dog that bit us. Collapsed into a poolside hammock, I was gradually restored to life by a frosty glass of Michelada: lager, lime juice, and spices, served over ice in a chalice with a salted rim.

There are different theories as to where the name *michelada* originates. One is that it derives from slang essentially meaning "my cold beer." Sometimes it's known simply as a *chelada*, though this can also refer to versions made only with beer and lime juice. Sometimes it's called a *Cubano*. All of these variations fall into the broad category of *cerveza preparada* (prepared beer). Nailing down a precise definition seems to be a lost cause.

Not that it matters. Like the Bloody Mary, the Michelada is infinitely variable according to personal preference. It can be as simple as lager, lime, and salt,

MICHELADA

Salt, for the glass rim

Lime wedge or wheel, for garnish

1 oz. fresh lime juice

3/4 tsp. hot sauce

5 dashes Maggi Jugo

12 oz. (360 ml) dark Mexican lager

Pour some salt onto a small plate wide enough to accommodate the rim of a beer glass. Moisten the rim of the glass with the lime wedge or wheel and coat it with the salt. Fill the glass about halfway with ice. Combine the lime juice, hot sauce, and Maggi in the glass, adding the beer last. Stir gently to combine. Garnish with the lime wedge.

Serves 1

or as weird as beer, gin, and Parmesan cheese (an actual recipe I came across in a Mexican cooking magazine).

It can use a light lager or something dark like Negro Modelo. Savory ingredients like Maggi seasoning, soy sauce, or Worcestershire sauce are optional, as are tomato juice and hot sauce.

This recipe is one that has served me well. Modify it with abandon. (See pages 95 and 97 for two worthy variations.)

BOILERMAKER

1 oz. whiskey

12 to 16 oz. (360 to 480 ml) lager or pale ale

Pour the whiskey into a shot glass and the beer into a pint glass. Drop the former into the latter, then drink gradually or all at once.

Serves 1

The standard Boilermaker—a shot of whiskey dropped into a glass of beer—brings to mind either hard-drinking, glassy-eyed inebriates or hard-working makers of actual boilers. Just how the name *Boilermaker* got attached to the practice of dropping a shot of whiskey into a glass of beer is unknown. Even the International Brotherhood of Boilermakers, Iron Ship Builders, Blacksmiths, Forgers, and Helpers doesn't know for sure, though they do venture a guess.

The union suggests that the name perhaps derived from an incident involving Richard Trevithick, who demonstrated in 1801 that a steam engine could provide power for passenger transportation with his "Puffing Devil" locomotive. Unfortunately, he and his crew left the boiler running while retiring to a local pub, and when the water ran out, the Puffing Devil caught fire. It's a cautionary tale about the dangers of careless imbibing, but does it have anything to do with the Boilermaker name? Maybe not, but all drinks benefit from a good story.

Regardless of where it came from, the combination of a beer and a shot is probably about as old as distillation. The Dutch have their *kopstootje*, or "little headbutt," a tulip glass of genever paired with lager. The Scandinavians have aquavit sipped next to stout. Americans poured rum into their ale and called it "calibogus." It doesn't require much stretching of the imagination to drop a shot of one into a glass of the other. The most popular combination today is an American whiskey such as bourbon, rye, or Tennessee whiskey dropped into a lager. For those who prefer something a little more flavorful, a pale ale works nicely too.

This is one of the simplest recipes in the book, yet also one of the most difficult to make. With just two ingredients, preparing the drink is easy. It's finding one of those ingredients that will take some work. But not to worry—there are acceptable substitutes that are much easier to acquire.

The elusive ingredient is Amer Picon, a bitter orange aperitif produced in Marseille, France. Created in 1837 by Gaétan Picon, one hundred years later his company could boast, *"Il n'est plus une partie du globe où n'ait pénétré le Picon!"* ("There isn't any part of the world where Picon hasn't penetrated!")

That, alas, is no longer true. Amer Picon has not been imported to the United States for a long time. Bottles are much sought after by American cocktail geeks, who make a point of smuggling a bottle back in their luggage on trips abroad. The liqueur is called for in classic cocktails like the Picon Punch, the Brooklyn, and the Picon Bière—a simple combination of lager or wheat beer with a shot of Amer Picon, essentially the sophisticated French cousin of the American Boilermaker.

Further complicating things is that Amer Picon itself has changed over the years. Originally produced at 39 percent alcohol by volume, it gradually dropped to just 18 percent. So even if one does manage to snag a bottle, it won't have quite the same alcoholic heft as it used to.

What to do? Second to booking a flight to Europe, the best bet is to replicate the bitter orange flavor of Amer Picon with more readily available ingredients.

PICON BIÈRE

1 oz. Amer Picon or other bitter orange liqueur

12 to 16 oz. (360 to 480 ml) lager or wheat beer

Pour the Amer Picon into a pint glass. Top it with the beer.

Serves 1

One of these is the domestically produced Torani Amer, which is higher in proof but inferior in flavor. Gran Classico or Amaro Cio-Ciaro, perhaps supplemented with a bit of orange liqueur, is another decent option. One can also search online for various do-it-yourself approaches to making Amer Picon replicas. While these can be good in a Picon Bière, the ones I've sampled seem to lack the certain *je ne sais quoi* of the original.

Fortunately, there's a new option. Bigallet Viriana China China is a spirit that has been produced in France since the 1870s but has just recently arrived in the United States. It's made by macerating bitter and sweet orange peels in alcohol, and at 80 proof it is approximately the same strength as the original Amer Picon. It's great on its own and mixed with beer, lending a pleasant bitter-orange flavor to a straightforward lager. A final option is Amer dit Picon, a replica produced by Golden Moon Distillery in Colorado, though I've not yet had the opportunity to try it.

BERLINER WEISSE MIT STRIPPE

About 1 oz.
kummel,
or to taste

12 to 16 oz.
(360 to 480 ml)
Berliner weisse

Pour the kummel into a
beer glass and top it with
the Berliner weisse.

Serves 1

The American lager Miller High Life proclaims itself "the Champagne of Beers," but this title should arguably go to Germany's Berliner weisse, a bright, effervescent, low-alcohol, and mildly sour beer brewed from barley and wheat. According to legend, Napoleon's troops found the drink so pleasing when they invaded Berlin in 1806 that they declared it "the Champagne of the north." With its crisp dryness and tart acidity, it's an apt comparison.

In the early twentieth century, Berlin boasted twenty breweries making its signature beer. Then falling demand, two world wars, and the Cold War conflict wiped out the industry. A few years ago, Berliner weisse was perilously close to extinction. Thankfully, it has recently enjoyed a small revival, both in Germany and among North American craft brewers.

Berliner weisse today is soured with a controlled fermentation of *Lactobacillus*, and fans of sour beers enjoy it without any additional flavorings. Earlier brewers had to contend with a more varied menagerie of microscopic invaders. It was probably due to this that the practice of enjoying the beer *mit schuss*—that is, with a little syrup to sweeten it—became standard. The two most popular of these syrups are *himbeer* (raspberry) and *waldmeister*, an alarmingly green herbal syrup flavored with woodruff. The latter can be ordered online in the United States. It's unique and definitely worth a try; a small vial appears in the photo opposite.

Then there's *Berliner weiss mit strippe*. That's the beer with a shot of liquor added to it. This is made with *korn*, a German spirit similar to an unaged whiskey, or *kummel*, a liqueur flavored with caraway and other herbs such as cumin and fennel. Partial though I am to drinking Berliner weisse unadulterated, I like it with the kummel too. It nicely counters the acidity and adds a very enjoyable savory note.

Kummels from Combier, Gilka, and a few other distillers are available on the American market, with Combier being my preferred brand.

Tracking down Berliner weisse may take some hunting. German brands may be found year-round. American versions are most likely to appear during the summer months. Look for Hottenroth from the Bruery or Oarsman from Bell's. The style has become especially popular in Florida, where brewers have taken to making "Florida Weisse" beers brewed with citrus and other fruits.

I learned of the *laternmaß* from my German friend Tobias Heinrich, who tells me that the drink is popular among young partygoers in southern Bavaria. Translated, the name means "lantern mug"; the "ß" is pronounced as a soft, long "s," roughly rhyming with "mass." It's made by lowering a stemmed glass of cherry liqueur into a stein of either German beer or a mixture of beer and lemon soda. The bright red liqueur surrounded by pale beer makes the glass resemble a lantern. As the drinker imbibes, the liqueur gradually flavors the beer.

I make it with Cherry Heering, a Scandinavian cherry liqueur that is widely available in the United States. For the beer, try a good lager, pale ale, or cream ale.

A German *maß* (stein) is technically defined as holding a liter in volume. That's a lot of beer! I've scaled the recipe down to sixteen ounces, but feel free to scale upward if you're thirsty and have an authentic *maß* on hand. And if you have the glassware, consider starting a *Maßkrugstemmen*, a competition to see who can last the longest holding a full stein of beer with their arm fully outstretched. The first to bend an elbow or spill the beer loses.

The *Laternmaß* is one of many variations on the same theme. The Snow Mug (*Schneemaß*) combines *korn* (a German distillate similar to unaged whiskey) with pale beer, lemonade, and vanilla ice cream. A Goat Mug (*Goaßmaß*) mixes dark lager or wheat beer with Coca-Cola and cherry liqueur, whiskey, or brandy.

The *Laternmaß*, with its striking appearance, is my favorite of these. It isn't going to win any mixology competitions, but it's easy drinking and makes for a fun party trick.

LATERNMASS

16 oz. (480 ml) lager, pale ale, or cream ale

1 oz. cherry liqueur

Fill a glass stein with beer. Pour the cherry liqueur into a stemmed shot or flute glass. Gently lower the glass into the beer, avoiding mixing the two liquids as much as possible.

Serves 1

"How many people, I wonder, are aware that Champagne and Guinness' Stout make one of the best combinations possible?" So asked Edward Spencer in his book *Cakes and Ale*, first published in 1897. At the time, the drink may have been esoteric. Popular lore claims that it was first served at the Brooks's Club in London in 1861 in honor of the recently deceased Prince Albert. Today, the drink is one of the better-known beer cocktails, going under the name Black Velvet.

The combination appears again in Charles Baker's *Jigger, Beaker, and Glass* under the name Mariveles Velvet. In his inimitable style, Baker recalls sipping these in sight of the dormant Mariveles volcano at the Manila Polo Club, where the crater perfectly frames the setting sun. He evidently enjoyed the drink: "It will save life, nourish, encourage and induce sleep in insomniacs."

Well, that's an awful lot to ask of a cocktail! Although beer and wine purists alike might scoff at the combination, I like the Black Velvet. This is no time to break open the finest Champagne, but do go for a good dry sparkling wine that you wouldn't mind drinking on its own, instead of cheap headache juice.

The classic stout used in this is Guinness, but I prefer something a little richer. When I'm making these at my home in Oregon, the Cavatica Stout from Fort George works wonderfully. Just be sure to pick something robust.

The final question about this drink is how to serve it. The tendency today is to pour a modest portion in a Champagne flute or coupe. Spencer suggested a pewter tankard and specially recommended the drink "as a between-the-acts refresher for the amateur actor." I say it all depends on how thirsty you are.

This recipe was written with a Champagne flute in mind, but a pint glass, coffee mug, pewter tankard, red Solo cup, or other vessel of your choosing could work just as well. Simply vary the serving size as desired or as governed by one's responsibilities, keeping the ratio intact.

BLACK VELVET

4 oz. (120 ml) stout

4 oz. (120 ml) brut sparkling wine

Combine the stout and sparkling wine in a Champagne flute, coupe, or other vessel. Stir gently to combine.

Serves 1

In my time making drinks in Portland, Oregon, I managed three different bar programs. The longest running of these jobs was my post at Metrovino, where I stayed for just shy of three years. That may not seem like much, but in an industry that sees constant churn and turnover, it was enough to qualify as a respectably long run. I bring that up to provide some context for one of the most remarkable bars in the world, the American Bar at the Savoy Hotel in London.

The American Bar opened in 1893. In the time since, it has had only eleven head bartenders. That is amazing! And so are the bartenders who have taken up the role. The most famous is Harry Craddock, who tended bar in the United States until Prohibition exiled him to Europe, which was bad news for America but good news for Britain. He authored the extremely influential *Savoy Cocktail Book*, a collection of the drinks served there. Craddock's successor, Eddie Clarke, gets credit for the cocktail below.

I came across his Guinness Cooler in *Booth's Handbook of Cocktails and Mixed Drinks*, a book by John Doxat published in 1965 to commemorate the 225th anniversary of the Booth's distilling company. This drink combines stout beer with the aromatized wine Dubonnet, the orange liqueur Cointreau, and crème de cacao. The drink falls a little on the sweet side and the combination of bitter stout with chocolate and orange works very well. As the name implies, Guinness was the preferred beer at the time, but a fuller-bodied stout stands up a little better to the liqueurs. This is one drink in which a hoppy style of dark beer provides a nice balance; try it with something like Victory's Storm King imperial stout.

The original formulation called for an apple peel garnish, but I suggest the aromatics of an orange peel.

GUINNESS COOLER

1 oz. Dubonnet Rouge

2/3 oz. Cointreau

2/3 oz. crème de cacao

6 oz. (180 ml) stout

Twist of orange peel, for garnish

Combine all the ingredients in a goblet with ice, adding the stout last. Stir gently and garnish with the orange peel.

Serves 1

DUBLIN DEPTH CHARGE

½ oz. Irish cream liqueur

½ oz. Irish whiskey

6 to 8 oz. (180 to 240 ml) Guinness or other Irish stout

Combine the Irish cream and Irish whiskey in a shot glass. Pour enough stout into a pint glass to submerge the shot glass that will soon be dropped into it. Drop the shot glass into the beer and consume immediately.

Serves 1

With its relatively recent creation, this drink stretches the limits of the definition of "vintage." It is, however, something of a modern classic—assuming a shot chugged by partying frat boys can be considered classic.

It's arguably one of the most popular beer cocktails in the world. There are just two problems with it: It curdles upon preparation, requiring the drinker to chug it rapidly, and it has a tasteless name.

The drink is widely known as an Irish Car Bomb, an allusion to acts of terrorism that rightly makes one wary of ordering it, especially in an Irish pub. Its origin is reportedly traced to Charlie Oat, former owner of a place called Wilson's Saloon in Norwich, Connecticut, in 1979.

Oat, for his part, regrets the name, which he doubtless could not have imagined would catch on the way it did. "Today I would take the name back," he told a local news station in 2010 after an Irish group protested the popularity of the drink. "Of course—there's no question about it."

It would be tempting to sweep this unfortunately christened cocktail into the dustbin of history, but let's give Mr. Oat credit where credit is due: This is a tasty concoction. It works. The urgent need to slam the drink before it curdles only adds to the fun. I've never had a bad night that involved drinking it. Some bad next mornings, yes, but never a bad night.

In the interest of preserving this cocktail, I suggest a renaming: the Dublin Depth Charge. It's alliterative, descriptive, and nods to the Irish provenance of the ingredients.

Most important, it's unlikely to offend—though the same might not be said of your behavior if you consume too many of them.

HOT HELPERS

tories abound of American drinkers being put off by the warm cask ales of England, which are actually served at a cool cellar temperature that only seems warm in comparison to the ice-cold lagers sold here. Advertising for mass-market beers often emphasizes coldness above all else. A recent innovation in beer marketing is a can boasting "Two-Stage Cold Activation" with strips that change color to indicate when the beer has reached cold and "supercold" temperatures, allowing the consumer to enjoy it at "the peak of refreshment."

In the modern context, an entire chapter devoted to beer drinks that are served hot will strike many readers as strange. Indeed, in the early stages of writing the book, my intent was to include only two or three hot beverages in the section on vintage drinks. But as I researched historic beer drinks more thoroughly, I realized that there was far more to warm beer drinks than I'd expected, a genre of libations that has been almost entirely forgotten in modern times. As I dug deeper into the recipes and re-created them at home, I concluded that this lost style of drink merited a chapter of its own.

A booklet published in England in 1724 goes so far as to argue that imbibing warm drinks is best for the health. Titled *Warm Beer; or, A Treatise, wherein is declared by many reasons, that beer so qualified, is far more wholesome than that which is drank cold with a confutation of such objections as are made against it* (titles were longer then), it makes for dry reading, but the argument stemmed from a belief that the stomach digested food by boiling it. Hot drinks, therefore, were better for digestion than cold ones. We know better now, but the appeal of hot ale drinks is still worth contemplating.

It helps to imagine the setting in which they were consumed, going back in time to before the invention of central heating. Picture a rural traveler taking a sleigh-load of crops to sell in the city, stopping to spend the night and warm his weary body at one of the many taverns along the way. Alice Morse Earle describes the scene in *Customs and Fashions in Old New England*:

[The] host made his profits from the liquor he sold and from the sleeping-room he gave. Sometimes the latter was simple enough. A great fire was built in the fireplace of either front room—the bar-room or parlor—and round it, in a semicircle, feet to the fire and heads on their rolled-up buffalo robes, slept the tired travelers....It was certainly a gay winter's scene as sleigh after sleigh dashed into the tavern barn or shed, and the stiffened driver, after "putting up" his steed, walked quickly to the bar-room, where sat the host behind his cage-like counter, where ranged the inspiring barrels of old Medford or Jamaica rum and hard cider.

On nights like those, an ice-cold taste of the Rockies was the last thing a drinker needed. A big mug of warm ale, sweetened with a little sugar, flavored with a dash of spice, and fortified with a splash of liquor, however, was just the ticket. Perhaps the drink would be thickened with egg, cream, or oats. These brews weren't just drinks; they were sustenance for a cold and weary traveler. Tavern owners had two main ways of heating ale. They didn't have modern gas or electric ranges, so all the heat had to come from the fire. The method that's remembered most today is the loggerhead or "flip-dog," a heavy metal rod that was kept in the fire and heated until red hot. The hot loggerhead would be plunged into a mug of ale, caramelizing the sugars, heating the liquid, and building a big, frothy head. (For more on this technique, see the Flip on page 63.)

The other common way of heating ale was to use a muller, a metal pot designed for warming ale in a fire. These came in two styles: One of these was a sort of boot shape, the "toe" of which could be stuck into a fire to warm the ale. The other was shaped like a deep cone that could be set down into coals. This latter device appears in Charles Dickens's *The Old Curiosity Shop* when a patron orders a pint of warm ale:

The landlord retired to draw the beer, and presently returning with it, applied himself to warm the same in a small tin vessel shaped funnel-wise, for the convenience of sticking it far down in the fire and getting at the bright places. This was soon done, and he handed it to Mr. Codlin with that creamy froth upon the surface which is one of the happy circumstances attendant upon mulled malt.

The website Old & Interesting documents another approach to heating beer, the German and Austrian *bierwarmer*. This was a glass or metal tube that was filled with boiling water and then put into one's mug. In later years, electric versions of the same tool were invented, although the fashion for using them has died out.

By 1893, W. T. Marchant was already lamenting the decline in popularity of these drinks in his book *In Praise of Ale*:

It is a matter of regret that some of the more comforting drinks have gone out of date. When beer was the staple drink, morning, noon, and night, it was natural that our ancestors would prefer their breakfast beer warm and their "night-caps" flavoured.

Heated beer drinks such as the Flip, Wassail, Mulled Ale, and the Dog's Nose continued to appear in drink books through the early twentieth century. When Charles Baker published his *Gentleman's Companion* in 1939, he included a section of "seventeen or so 'Hot Helpers' calculated to keep chill swamp mists at bay, banish the megrims and warm body, heart & soul into a fine & amiable disposition." Four of Baker's Hot Helpers were made with beer, so this chapter borrows the name in honor of his contribution to keeping warm beer cocktails alive.

Hot beer drinks show up occasionally in later books, but one gets the impression that their inclusion became something of a formality, with the recipes lingering on like ghosts. They are rarely served in modern bars, which no longer have raging fires warming their patrons or iron loggerheads standing ready to froth a flip. Contemporary bars are very good at chilling drinks and often have elaborate ice programs. But heating drinks? At most bars there may be hot water or steam from an espresso or coffee machine, or perhaps a hot plate. The options are a lot more limited.

Warm drinks are one genre in which the mastery and creativity of bartenders of earlier centuries tends to surpass our own. Heated ale drinks are rare finds on today's menus, but they are well suited to the colder months. They deserve a place alongside the Hot Toddy, Hot Buttered Rum, and Tom and Jerry as classic warmers to imbibe on a chilly winter night.

Fortunately, the hot ale drinks of yore can be re-created with standard kitchen equipment, although I go into a few other methods as well (see page 26 for a discussion of sous vide). Heating ale in a pot on a kitchen range is just fine. The key is to heat it gradually and prevent it from becoming too hot, so having a thermometer on hand is useful. Excessive heating will accentuate bitterness and make the drink too hot to consume. In my experience, 140°F (60°C) is a good target temperature.

Finding the right beer is also important. The beers of earlier times were malt-driven, perhaps retaining a little more residual sugar than modern beers, and were not hopped as aggressively as contemporary ales. Even supposedly malty American ales tend to be liberally flavored with hops, although there are exceptions. For the most part, I find that Scottish and English ales are the best bet for these drinks. Though certainly not traditional, Belgian *quadrupels* can work well too.

My go-to beer for hot ale drinks is Samuel Smith's Winter Welcome, a malty English ale that, as the name implies, only comes out in the winter. But when else would one be making these drinks?

Some other good options are Robinson's Old Tom, Greene King Abbot Ale, Belhaven Scotch Ale, Great Divide Claymore Scotch Ale, Traquair House Ale, Hen's Tooth, and Old Speckled Hen. Rich barrel-aged ales like Samuel Smith's Yorkshire Stingo and J. W. Lees Harvest Ale also work nicely, but not nearly so well as to justify the expense of mixing them into cocktails. (Though by all means, do buy those beers and enjoy them as intended. They're wonderful.)

The drinks in this chapter can be a little tricky to make, and some of them are downright weird. Yet there is a reason people enjoyed them for centuries. Made correctly, they're very tasty. Charles Baker thought that his Hot Helpers would be the most valuable drinks in his book:

For when a man is wet and chilled through, blue with cold and long exposure in such voluntary tortures as November duck blinds, the wheel of an ocean-going sailing craft in a winter chance, or in any chilly and depleted situation, a Hot Helper will in 5 short minutes recall him from being a sorry and useless thing into restoration as a warm-hearted homebody, kind to dogs, children, wives, and even landlords.

With a testimonial like that, how can one resist? Give the drinks in this chapter a try and revive a bit of lost drinking history.

With the assistance of an older friend or a fake ID, college students today can purchase a keg of cold, fizzy beer just by visiting a liquor store. It wasn't always this easy. Before the days of cheap refrigeration, beer required tending. It was alive. A cask of ale had to be treated properly or else it would spoil.

Cedric Dickens, great-grandson of Charles Dickens, knew that a college keg party required care and preparation. While attending Eton and Cambridge, he learned the valuable skill of keeping a cask of ale in good condition.

"We kept the beer in our hot and smoky sitting-room," he recalled in *Drinking with Dickens*. "To counter the atmosphere, the first man back after the holidays was responsible for getting in two small barrels, covering them with damp cloths on which he sowed cress. Three days later mustard seed was added and allowed to germinate." The layer of cress and mustard kept the ale cool, protecting it from the depredations of heat and pipe-smoking college students.

When the ale was at its prime, "invitations were then issued to particular friends to join a select first-of-the-term party—the girls to eat mustard and cress sandwiches, the men to drink the clearest, coolest glass of amber ale ever drawn—ale fit for young Charles himself." One hopes for everyone's sake that they poured some ale for the women too.

This was the practice at summer parties. In winter they instead mulled the ale, infusing a stronger beer with spices, sweetening it, and serving it hot. Quaffing a mug of mulled ale with Cedric Dickens and his Cambridge pals must have been a treat. We can't re-create the company, but we can take a stab at the drink. The recipe here is based on Cedric's recipe, to which I've taken the liberty of adding a wheel of orange. It needn't be followed exactly. As long as the elements of malty ale, winter spices, sugar, and brandy are in place, it should come out very nicely.

MULLED ALE

12 oz. (360 ml) English-style ale

About 1 1/2 tbsp. brown sugar, or to taste

Pinch of ground cloves

Pinch of ground ginger

Pinch of ground cinnamon

Pinch of freshly grated nutmeg

2 oz. (60 ml) cognac

1 thin orange wheel

In a pot, combine the ale, sugar, and spices and heat them over medium heat to about 140°F (60°C). Pour them into a large warmed mug along with the cognac and orange wheel.

Serves 1

DOG'S NOSE

12 oz. (360 ml) porter

About 1 1/2 tbsp. brown sugar, or to taste

1 1/2 oz. genever or Old Tom gin

Freshly grated nutmeg, for garnish

In a pot, gently heat the porter over medium heat to about 140°F (60°C), stirring the sugar into it while it heats. Pour the genever or gin into a warmed mug, then add the porter. Garnish with a fresh grating of nutmeg.

Serves 1

The Dog's Nose is a drink that appears in Charles Dickens's first novel, *The Pickwick Papers*. In a scene set in a pub, a member of the local branch of the United Grand Junction Ebenezer Temperance Association reports on the month's new converts to the alcohol-free lifestyle. The first of these is H. Walker, a tailor with a wife and two children, who finds himself out of work and penniless.

Walker was formerly a habitual drinker of beer and ale. He claimed to "twice a week, for twenty years, taste 'dog's nose,' which your committee find upon inquiry, to be compounded of warm porter, moist sugar, gin, and nutmeg." It was perhaps under the influence of one of these potent pints that Walker was stuck with a rusty needle, causing him to lose the use of his right hand and hence his livelihood. Reformed by the accident, the newly temper-ate Walker "has nothing but cold water to drink, and never feels thirsty."

With such a wonderful pedigree, I knew that I wanted to include the Dog's Nose in this book. The problem was my early attempts at making the drink never turned out very well. I've experimented with it as far back as 2007, and while it made for an interesting literary allusion, it never appealed to me as anything more than a curiosity. It was certainly not the sort of thing I could picture anyone drinking twice a week for twenty years.

I was obviously doing something wrong, and revisiting the drink a few years later I figured out what it was. I was using the wrong gin. Dickens wrote *The Pickwick Papers* in 1836, which was a very interesting time in the history of distillation. Throughout the 1700s, England had suffered a "Gin Craze" as cheap, high-proof, low-quality gin swept the nation. As recounted in Lesley Jacobs Solmonson's informative *Gin: A Global History,* London in the 1730s was annually producing fourteen gallons of gin per resident. By 1750, the number of licensed gin retailers in London had swelled to 29,000. Life in eighteenth-century London was full of hardship, and the poor understandably eased their pains with inebriation. (Beer, in contrast, was viewed as a wholesome beverage. A 1751 pair of prints titled *Beer Street* and *Gin Lane* depict the stereotypical impressions of the two drinks. On Beer Street everyone is healthy and happy. On Gin Lane, everyone is drunk, impoverished, and reckless.)

By the 1830s, gin production had begun to shift to a higher-quality product. London distillers began making what we might today recognize as an "Old Tom"-style gin, which shares some of the botanical complexity of London dry with a sweeter body. This was sold to pubs by the barrel and would have had some sugar added to make it more palatable.

Another important development of 1830 was Aeneas Coffey's patent on the column still. Prior to this, English producers used pot stills to produce gins similar in style, though usually much inferior to, Dutch genever. This new method of distillation allowed for the production of cleaner, more neutral spirits, leading to the eventual development of the London dry gins we know today. Though wonderful in a martini, these are not the sorts of gins the cast of a Dickens novel would have used to spike their porter.

Fortunately, quality versions of genever and Old Tom gin have arrived on the American market in the years since I made my first Dog's Nose. Either of these works much better in the drink. Genever will give it a pleasing background maltiness and Old Tom will give it a slightly more assertive botanical aroma. Which to use is a matter of personal preference. Both do better than a dry gin.

With the gin covered, how about the porter? As with many of the cocktails in this chapter, English brands are the most reliable bet. American porters tend to be a little heavier on the hops, though there are exceptions. Try to find a porter that is not too bitter and has a good, malty body. The best selections I've found so far are Anchor Porter from San Francisco and the Taddy Porter from Samuel Smith in England.

Of all the hot ale drinks, none is remembered so well as wassail. The word conjures up images of happy carolers traveling from door to door, spreading holiday cheer as they sipped from warm mugs. But it's mostly the word *wassail* that is remembered. So what was it? Recipes vary widely, but generally speaking, it was a variety of mulled cider or ale.

Wassailing is now associated with Christmas, but its roots are likely pre-Christian. The word derives from the Anglo-Saxon toast *waes hael*, meaning "be in good health." The proper response to this was *drinc hael*, a toast to one's health, which led, of course, to drinking.

Some forms of wassailing would have been performed for trees, not people, to ensure a good apple harvest. Wassailing was also a kind of charity. The poor would go from house to house, asking for wassail and food, offering in exchange their goodwill and song. An example of the latter gives a clue to the recipe:

*Wassail, wassail, all over the town
Our toast it is white and our ale it is brown
Our bowl it is made of the white maple tree
With the wassailing bowl, we'll drink to thee.*

The role of the brown beer is obvious, but the white toast requires some explanation. Floating toasts of dense bread in punch was once a common practice. Drinkers today may prefer to skip the toast and opt for roasted apples; slicing an orange into thin wheels is an even simpler garnish.

WASSAIL

1 qt. (960 ml) English ale

12 oz. (360 ml) cream sherry

About ½ cup (110 g) packed brown sugar, or to taste

Peel of 1 lemon

Juice of 1 lemon (about 1 ½ oz.)

1 tsp. ground cinnamon

1 tsp. freshly grated nutmeg

1 tsp. ground ginger

2 roasted apples or fresh sliced oranges

Combine everything but the apples in a large pot and heat over medium heat to about 140°F (60°C). Remove from the heat, add the apples or oranges, and serve in warmed mugs.

Serves 6 to 8

This recipe is adapted from the charmingly titled *Cooling Cups and Dainty Drinks,* an 1869 book of recipes written by William Terrington. Terrington's book provides an in-depth look at beer drinks as they were made in the mid-1800s. The addition of moderately sweet, nutty sherry adds a wonderful richness to the drink.

FLIP

12 oz. (360 ml) English-style ale

Boiling water

1 ½ tbsp. Demerara sugar

1 oz. high-proof
rum

In a pot, heat the ale over medium heat to about 140°F (60°C). Warm a tempered glass mug with boiling water. Discard the water and immediately add the sugar, rotating the mug so that the sugar coats the sides of the mug. Add the rum, tilt the mug so that it reaches the edge of the glass to facilitate setting it aflame, and ignite the rum with a match or lighter. Holding the mug by the handle, rotate the mug and allow the flame to gradually caramelize the sugar. Pour the hot ale into the mug, extinguishing the flame (as shown on page 65). Allow the mug to cool to a safe temperature before drinking.

Serves 1

The Europeans who settled the northeastern United States had a mighty thirst for rum. Colonial Americans knocked back gallons of pure alcohol each year. A lot of this was rum, and a lot of this rum was poured into a drink called the Flip.

The days are short, the
weather's cold,
By tavern fires tales are told.
Some ask for dram when
they first come in,
Others with flip and bounce begin.

That's from a 1704 almanac, reproduced in drink historian Wayne Curtis's book *And a Bottle of Rum: A History of the World in Ten Cocktails*, in which he describes the popularity of the Flip as bordering on a mania.

The recipe for a basic flip called for just three ingredients: rum, ale, and a sweetener such as sugar or molasses. It's the method of preparation that made the drink unique. Tavern owners adapted the loggerhead—a long iron tool with a bulbous head used for melting tar pitch—to heat drinks instead. The loggerhead would be kept in the tavern fire, then plunged into a tankard of flip, causing it to heat up and build a big, frothy head. It also caramelized the sugar, giving the drink a bittersweet flavor.

Colonial Americans drank flips in astonishing quantities. Curtis writes that flip tumblers of the era held up to a gallon each. One can imagine that so much alcohol often caused disputes in taverns to end with physical blows—from which we get the phrase "at loggerheads" to describe a conflict.

The traditional Flip is a delicious drink, but re-creating it in modern times can be a bit tricky. I have tried it out with a loggerhead that Portland blacksmith Nathan Zilka fashioned for me (the metal tool in the photo on page 62), and it is a fun experience. Dave Arnold, the inventive mind behind the bar Booker and Dax in New York, has gone so far as to fabricate his own electric Red Hot Poker, which he heats to 1,700°F (930°C) before plunging it into drinks. But not everyone has a fireplace, much less an iron loggerhead.

I've come up with a more practical method inspired by a popular Portland cocktail called a Spanish Coffee. In this drink, a tempered glass mug is given a sugar rim, then high-proof rum and orange liqueur are ignited in the glass. The flames gradually caramelize the sugar, then a stream of coffee liqueur is added, and finally all is extinguished with a pour of hot coffee. Whipped cream and a grating of spice complete the drink. At its birthplace, Hubers Café, the bartenders and waitstaff have the process of making Spanish Coffees down to a deftly executed routine.

At my own bars, where we did not always prepare for Spanish Coffees, unexpected orders of this complicated drink were the bane of my existence. However, I later realized that the Spanish Coffee method could be used to replicate the burnt sugar character of a flip made with a metal poker. Flames from ignited rum can be used to caramelize sugar in a mug, and then ale warmed on a stove can be poured in to put out the fire. It's not quite as dramatic as plunging a red-hot loggerhead into a giant tankard, but it gets the job done.

Make this drink with a good English ale; my favorite for this is Samuel Smith's Winter Welcome. For the rum, choose a high-proof Jamaican like Smith & Cross. It has the alcohol content to ignite easily and complex aromatics that combine beguilingly with caramelized sugar and warm ale.

As always when making cocktails that involve flame, care must be taken to avoid injury. Use a preheated, tempered glass mug to avoid having it shatter. Prepare the drink away from anything flammable, preferably over a metal sink. And finally, be sure to allow the glass to cool sufficiently before touching it with one's hand or lips.

A cocktail of just rum, sugar, and warm beer may not sound like much, but somehow the Flip adds up to much more than the sum of its parts. I argue you to give it a try to see why so many early American tavern-goers couldn't get enough of it.

RUM FLIP

2 large eggs

16 oz. (480 ml) English-style ale

1 tbsp. sugar

½ tsp. freshly grated nutmeg

2 oz. (60 ml) rum

In a warm bowl or pitcher, beat the eggs with a splash of ale, the sugar, and the nutmeg. Add the rum. In a pot, gently heat the remaining ale over medium heat to about 140°F (60°C). Gradually add it to the egg mixture, beating with a fork or whisk all the while. Pour the mixture back and forth between two pitchers until it is smooth, then pour through a fine-mesh strainer and serve in warm mugs.

Serves 2 or 3

The simple Flip described on pages 63 and 64 inspired more elaborate variations, often flavored with spices or made creamy with the addition of whole eggs. Eventually egg became the defining feature of the drink. Contemporary use of the word *flip* denotes pretty much any cocktail with a whole egg in it, usually served cold and often without any beer or rum at all. A few contemporary flips appear in the final chapter of this book (see the Averna Stout Flip on page 149).

By the time Jerry Thomas compiled his *Bar-Tender's Guide* in 1862, the Flip had taken a step closer to our modern interpretation of the drink. Thomas's book provides recipes for six flips,

five of which call for eggs. Four of them call for ale, showing that beer was still an important, though optional, part of the drink.

Technique had evolved too, with the glowing-hot loggerhead replaced by simply warming the ale by the fire. The warmed ale was then poured into a pitcher with beaten eggs, sugar, spices, and rum or brandy. "The essential in 'flips' of all sorts," Thomas wrote, "is . . . to produce the smoothness by repeated pouring back and forth between two vessels, and beating up the eggs well in the first instance."

Following the instructions is important; I was a bit careless in my first attempt and ended up with what can only be described as hot beer and scrambled eggs. Not recommended.

The two important steps to get right are the gradual incorporation of the ale and the pouring back and forth of the flip. When pouring the warm beer into the egg mixture, do so gradually and continue beating the eggs as the ale pours; it may help as well to beat a little cold ale into the eggs before warming the beer. For the vessels in which to pour the flip back and forth, use steel bowls, insulated cocktail shakers, or large steel pitchers of the sort that baristas use to steam milk. Warm them with hot water first so that they don't cool down the drink. If done correctly, the repeated pouring back and forth will make the flip "as smooth as cream." (The appearance of this smooth liquid pouring back and forth led to the drink also being called a Yard of Flannel.)

Odd as this drink may sound, it has a warmth and richness that makes it very enticing. Jerry Thomas suggests its use as a cold remedy, but I enjoy it any time the weather turns chilly.

For the beer, use a mild English ale; this is a good drink for Old Speckled Hen, for instance. For the rum, I'm once again drawn to a strong naval-style rum like Smith & Cross.

The recipe here follows Thomas's Rum Flip almost exactly. The only major change is that he called for a quart of ale. I've halved the quantities of everything to produce a more reasonable volume; it's still plenty to serve two or three people.

RUMFUSTIAN

2 egg yolks

10 oz. (300 ml) English-style ale

1 tbsp. brown sugar

1/4 tsp. freshly grated nutmeg

1/4 tsp. ground cinnamon

2 oz. (60 ml) genever or Old Tom gin

6 oz. (180 ml) cream sherry

In a warm bowl or pitcher, beat the egg yolks with a splash of ale, the sugar, nutmeg, cinnamon, and genever or gin. In a pot, gently heat the sherry and remaining ale over medium heat to about 140°F (60°C). Gradually add the sherry mixture to the egg mixture, beating with a fork or whisk all the while. Pour the mixture back and forth between two pitchers until it is smooth, then pour through a fine mesh strainer and serve in warm mugs.

Serves 2 or 3

Rumfustian "is the singular name bestowed upon a drink very much in vogue with English sportsmen, after their return from a day's shooting." So wrote Jerry Thomas in his *Bar-Tender's Guide*.

Surprisingly, the Rumfustian doesn't contain any rum. It's essentially a flip made with sherry and gin; given the timing of the book's publication, the gin would have likely been an Old Tom or genever rather than a spirit similar to today's London dry.

A very similar drink from the same period was Purl. Originally made by infusing ale with wormwood, it evolved into a warm ale drink mixed with gin, sugar, and spices, much like the Dog's Nose (page 59) or Mulled Ale (page 56). Purl-men sold it to workers from boats on the Thames River.

A modern interpretation of the drink can now be found at Purl, a cocktail bar in London.

Featuring all of these drinks separately would be redundant, so this adaptation of Rumfustian will have to stand in for the lot. I've scaled it down to more manageable portions from Thomas's recipe, which called for the yolks of twelve eggs and a quart of ale. I've also varied the means of preparation just a little, making it much like the Rum Flip (page 67). The recipe here maintains the spirit of the original and pleasingly balances the sherry, gin, and ale.

According to *Oxford Night Caps*, "Such is the intoxicating property of this liquor, that none but hard drinkers will venture to regale themselves with it a second time." Consider yourself warned.

Lamb's Wool (page 72)

Next crowne the bowle full
With gentle Lambs wooll,
Adde sugar, nutmeg, and ginger,
With store of ale too,
And thus ye must doe
To make the Wassaile a swinger.

That verse, providing the recipe for Lamb's Wool, comes from the seventeenth-century poet Robert Herrick's "Twelfth Night; or, King and Queen," a poem portraying wassail festivities. Indeed, Lamb's Wool is "merely a variety of Wassail Bowl," writes Richard Cook rather dismissively in *Oxford Night Caps*. Evidently the drink wasn't very popular at Oxford; however, it did catch on elsewhere in England and Ireland.

The key ingredient in Lamb's Wool is pulped roasted apples, which are added to warm ale with sugar and spices. The apple rises to the surface of the hot drink, gradually sinking as it cools. Traditionally it would be made in large batches for a group. I've scaled down the recipe so that it can be made *à la minute* for one, and changed the spice to cinnamon. I also suggest adding a shot of bourbon, because with cinnamon and roasted apples in the drink, it would be a crime not to. Omit the bourbon for a more authentic re-creation.

Some have speculated that the name *Lamb's Wool* comes from the fluffy appearance of the apple puree on the surface of the drink. Richard Cook suggests that the name is a corruption of the Celtic *la mas ubal*, the "day of the apple fruit," a winter celebration of the angel presiding over fruits and seeds. Regardless of where the name comes from, it's an unusual drink that merits a revival, perfect for an autumn day when the temperature is falling, apples are ripe, and leaves are turning color. A rich, malty ale is what's called for here. Samuel Smith's Winter Welcome is a seasonally appropriate choice.

LAMB'S WOOL

12 oz. (360 ml) English-style ale

3 tbsp. Spiced Apple Puree, *see recipe below*

1 tbsp. brown sugar

1 ½ oz. bourbon (optional)

Cinnamon stick, for grating

In a pot, heat the ale, apple puree, and sugar over medium heat to about 140°F (60°C). Remove from the heat and pour the mixture into a warmed mug, along with the bourbon (if using). Garnish with freshly grated cinnamon.

Serves 1

SPICED APPLE PUREE

4 apples

4 oz. (120 ml) apple cider

2 tsp. ground cinnamon

Preheat the oven to 300°F (150°C). Peel and roughly chop the apples into 1-inch (2.5-cm) cubes, trimming any fibrous bits near the core. Place them in a baking dish with the cider and cinnamon. Cover and bake for 1 to 1 ½ hours, until soft. Puree with a blender, mash by hand, or press the apples through a potato ricer to make a smooth puree. Store it in a sealed container in the refrigerator for up to 1 week.

Makes about 2 cups (480 ml)

ROYAL POSSET

1 pt. (480 ml) cream

8 oz. (240 ml) ale

2 tbsp. sugar

3 egg yolks, beaten

2 egg whites, beaten

Freshly grated nutmeg

Rum (optional)

In a pot, combine the cream and ale, then add the sugar, egg yolks and whites, and a generous grating of nutmeg. Whisk everything together thoroughly. Gently heat the mixture over medium heat, stirring as it warms. As it approaches boiling, the posset will thicken. Remove the pot from the heat before the mixture comes to a boil.

The posset can be served as-is in a bowl and ladled into warmed cups, or poured through a fine-mesh strainer to remove the curds. (Strained, it will yield about 2 cups/480 ml.)

If desired, pour about 1 ounce rum into a warmed mug and top with about 6 ounces (180 ml) Royal Posset.

Serves 2 or 3

With a modern cocktail renaissance that relentlessly raids the past for inspiration, might a revival of posset be the next big thing? Probably not, but making it is a fun way to step back in time.

Reader, I'm not going to lie. This is a weird drink. As if this chapter's exploration of hot beer and eggs wasn't already strange enough (see page 67), the Posset takes things to the next level by adding milk or cream and intentionally making it curdle. Posset was meant to be as much a meal as a drink. Curdled milk doesn't appeal to us today, but a few centuries ago it would have been too nutritious for frugal housekeep-ers to waste. Don't be put off by the strange procedure. This drink is actually very enjoyable, with a richness comparable to eggnog.

The traditional way to serve this would be in a posset pot, a vessel with an open top and a spout that reaches to the bottom. This allowed a person to draw liquid from the bottom for drinking and to skim curds off the top for eating with a spoon. (The pot in the photo on page 74, while not an authentic posset pot, approximates the setup.)

The drink was well known enough to appear in the plays of Shakespeare. With the help of posset, Lady Macbeth drugs the guards of King Duncan to put

them to sleep while the couple commits murder. In *Hamlet*, *posset* finds use as a verb when the ghost of the deceased king describes the poison that took his life:

That swift as quicksilver it
courses through
The natural gates and alleys of
the body,
And with a sudden vigor doth posset
And curd, like eager droppings
into milk,
The thin and wholesome blood;
so did it mine

Odd as it may sound to intentionally curdle milk, related "milk punch" enjoyed a century or so of popularity beginning in the mid-1700s. This was made by adding warm milk to punch; the milk would curdle when it reacted with juice from lemons or limes in the punch. The curds would then be strained off and the clear liquid bottled and stored. The milk eased the acidity of the citrus, and with the solids removed the bottled punch could be kept indefinitely.

Lacking access to an antique posset pot and having little desire to eat spoonfuls of curd, I like to take a similar approach by straining the curds out before drinking. Readers desiring the full old-timey experience can consume it curds and all.

Posset was so common that *The Practical Housewife* of 1860 collected eleven different recipes for it. Ale Posset was simply boiled milk mixed with mild ale, toasted bread, sugar, and nutmeg. Others were more elaborate. Jelly Posset brought eggs and cinnamon into the mixture. Orange Posset called for Seville orange, sweet and bit-ter almonds, brandy, and wine. Sack Posset was made with Spanish wine and crumbled biscuits. These possets were accompanied by various recipes for caudles, flips, and purls. Warm, nourishing beer drinks were prepared in seemingly endless variety.

I'm partial to the Royal Posset, which combines ale with rich, heavy cream. It's a mild drink, so although it's not in the original recipe, I like adding a good English-style rum to it as well. Pusser's does nicely.

HOT SCOTCHY

8 oz. (240 ml) Wort, *see recipe below*

1 ½ oz. Scotch

Whipped cream (optional)

In a pot, heat the wort over medium heat to between 140 and 150°F (60 to 65°C). Pour it into a warmed mug and add the Scotch. Top with whipped cream, if desired.

Serves 1

WORT

1 gal. (3.8 L) water

2 lbs. (910 g) two-row pale malt, milled

1 lb. (455 g) crystal 20L malt, milled, *see Note*

Warm an insulated cooler with hot water. In a pot, heat the water over medium or high heat to between 165 and 170°F (70 to 75°C). Place both malts in a fine-mesh bag. Empty the cooler, then pour the heated water into it. Lower the mesh bag into the water, gathering the top so that the grain does not spill out. Stir it with a large spoon to ensure that there are no dry clumps of grain. Probe the mixture with a thermometer, making sure it reaches at least 150°F (65°C). If it hasn't, add a small amount of boiling water to bring up its temperature. Seal the cooler and allow the grains to steep for 45 minutes.

Remove the grain bag, squeezing gently to extract the liquid, and pour the wort into a pot. Bring it to a boil on the stove, allowing the liquid to reduce to between 7 and 8 cups (1.7 to 2 L) of liquid. The more it reduces, the more concentrated and sweet the wort will become. Taste frequently; it should end up sweet and malty, but not cloying. If not used immediately, the wort can be stored in a sealed container in the refrigerator for 3 to 5 days.

Makes 7 to 8 cups (1.7 to 2 L)

Note: The "20L" refers to degree of roast.

This is the only drink in the book that doesn't use beer. Instead it uses wort, the liquid extraction of barley that turns into beer after yeast, hops, and time do their work. It's hot, sweet, and malty, and when spiked with Scotch it becomes absolutely delicious. Upon trying this Hot Scotchy for the first time, beer writer Jeff Alworth proclaimed it, with perhaps just a hint of exaggeration, "the finest beverage known to man."

The drink has floated under the radar until now, mainly because beer brewers and their friends were the only ones able to drink it. Stores sell beer, not wort (although I have this dream that an entrepreneurial Portlandian will someday open a truck dispensing hot wort and mini Scotch bottles). To make wort, you pretty much have to go all-in on making beer. That's a lot of effort just to have a cocktail.

My friend Ezra Johnson-Greenough introduced me to the drink and helped arrange for Yetta Vorobik to serve it at the Hop and Vine with wort borrowed from Upright Brewing. When we needed more wort to feature it at one of our Brewing Up Cocktails events, Ezra scaled down the Upright recipe for use at the bar. Finally, with this book coming into print, Ezra and I figured out a way to make reasonable quantities of wort at home using standard kitchen tools and malted barley purchased from a homebrew store. It's much easier, and requires much less specialized gear, than becoming a full-on homebrewer.

Even so, having a basic knowledge of how beer is brewed will help you with this recipe. To make beer, the starches in barley malt have to be converted into sugar; this is done by steeping the grains in hot water, a process known as mashing. After mashing, the spent grains are strained off and the liquid left behind is wort. Brewers would boil this and add hops and yeast to make beer. Making wort for a Hot Scotchy, we get to skip those steps.

If you were making beer, care would be taken to achieve just the right extraction. This recipe requires a lot less precision, because we're not turning it into a finished beer. We're just heating up the malty liquid and adding Scotch.

The recipe here is pretty basic. Ezra notes that it could be tweaked with the use of other grains, such as adding some chocolate malt for a roasty nuttiness. The real key is making sure that the mash hits at least 150°F (65°C) to ensure the conversion of the starches into sugar.

Choosing the right Scotch is a matter of preference. I like a good blend or an unpeated single malt, like Macallan. A peaty Islay malt like Ardbeg will take the drink in a smoky direction. Yetta likes to top the drink with a dollop of fresh whipped cream, a decadent and tasty addition.

The malt and fine-mesh bag needed for the wort recipe can be purchased at any homebrew store, where they will also mill the grain.

HOT BRUIN

1 (750-ml) bottle Rodenbach Grand Cru

3/4 oz. maple syrup

1 cinnamon stick

1 star anise

8 juniper berries

4 whole cloves

Peel from 1 orange

4 oz. (120 ml) aquavit

3/4 oz. maraschino liqueur

Orange wheels, for garnish

Combine all the ingredients except the aquavit, maraschino, and orange wheels in a pot. Heat the mixture over medium heat to about 140°F (60°C), cover the pot, and reduce the heat to very low. Allow the mixture to infuse for about 10 minutes. Remove the spices, if desired, pour in the aquavit and maraschino, and ladle the Hot Bruin into warmed mugs. Garnish each drink with an orange wheel.

Serves 4 to 6

Contemporary warm beer cocktails are few and far between. One of the few I've come across is the Glueh Kriek from Cascade Brewing, a Portland brewery specializing in sour barrel-aged beers. They combine their aged, cherry-flavored sour ale with winter spices and serve it hot, to very good effect. I've heard of Belgian breweries making similar ales and have come across references to Calibou, an old warm drink made with lambic, sugar, cinnamon, cloves, and eggs, although I'm not aware of anyone serving it in modern times.

These drinks inspired me to take my own shot at making a modern hot beer cocktail. Rather than a fruit lambic, I reached for Flanders brown ale, a sour style originating from the Flemish region of Belgium. The brand called for here, Rodenbach Grand Cru, is a blend of barrel-aged and new ale, and is less assertively tart than some other beers in this style. (The classic Rodenbach contains a lower proportion of aged beer but can also be used in this drink.) I use the barrel-aged Linie aquavit from Norway as the primary spirit, although other brands of aquavit can certainly be substituted.

CONTEMPORARY
COCKTAILS

The drinks included in the book so far have relied on pretty standard beers: mild ales and porters, crisp lagers and pilsners, and the occasional classic sour beer from Germany or Belgium. This chapter continues to use these, but also takes full advantage of the great range of beers now available thanks to the revival of craft brewing. Intensely hoppy IPA, refreshing hefeweizen, fruity lambic, smoky rauchbier, spiced witbier, aromatic saison—all beers are welcome in the modern beer cocktail.

This chapter also uses the full arsenal of spirits available in a modern bar. There's the usual rum, whiskey, gin, and brandy, but also Chartreuse, Galliano, mezcal, Aperol, and more. The techniques get more creative too. Turning beer into flavorful syrups? Sure! Making jam with raspberries and lambic? Yes! Garnishing a drink with ground-up chiles, salt, and worms? Definitely!

Contemporary mixology is not afraid to get weird. Many have said we are experiencing the second golden age of cocktails, and I completely agree with them. The range of ingredients available, the knowledge and passion of bartenders, and the creativity exhibited behind the bar today are unparalleled. And if this creativity sometimes leads to a recipe that seems strange or complex, rest assured that the end goal of the drinks in this book is always deliciousness.

Some of the cocktails in this chapter are as easy to make as pouring beer and spirits in a glass. Others take a bit more preparation. The range of flavors and styles is immense. That bartenders who consume shots of Fernet-Branca after their shift find bitter IPA cocktails like the Blanket Finish (page 146) appealing should come as no surprise, but there are also sweet drinks like the Zelda (page 107), tart drinks like the Portland Rickey (page 133), and spicy drinks like the Piña Pica (page 95). Like a skilled bartender, this chapter is ready with something for everyone.

GREEN DEVIL

Absinthe

1 oz. gin

About 11 oz. (330 ml) Duvel or other Belgian-style golden ale

Lightly rinse the inside of a Duvel chalice or other glass with absinthe, discarding the excess. Add the gin and then top it off with the Duvel, allowing a large head to form.

Serves 1

This chapter begins fittingly with the drink that first sparked my interest in beer cocktails, the Green Devil, from Canadian beer writer Stephen Beaumont. Back in 2008, when I was transitioning from working at a think tank in Washington, D.C., to a bar in Portland, Oregon, Stephen presented a seminar at Tales of the Cocktail in New Orleans called "How to View Beer as an Ingredient Rather than as the Drink unto Itself." A bit wordy as a title, but otherwise a good description of this book.

I don't remember all of the drinks served at that seminar, but this one stood out. The cocktail takes its name from two of its ingredients: absinthe, also known as the Green Fairy, and Duvel, which means "devil" in a Flemish dialect. At a robust 8.5 percent alcohol by volume, this Belgian golden ale hardly calls out for additional booze. However, the result in this instance is sufficiently tasty to make risking the

hangover worthwhile; a one-drink limit is advisable.

The Green Devil is all about emphasizing aromatics. Pouring the beer aggressively into the glass builds a sizable head, lifting the aromas of absinthe and dry gin. Serving it in a proper Duvel chalice or other tulip-shaped glass enhances these even more. If this type of glass is unavailable, any wide-mouthed glass that allows a large head to form will work just fine.

Duvel currently exports bottles to the United States in volumes of 330 ml (11.2 ounces) and 750 ml (25 ounces). The former size is perfect for this drink.

According to urban legend, the Galliano-spiked Harvey Wallbanger cocktail earned its moniker by the effect it had on a California surfer named Tom Harvey. Harvey was said to consume them at Hollywood's Blackwatch Bar in the 1950s, getting so blitzed that by the end of the night he'd be found banging his head into the walls.

As with many stories in the alcohol business, the truth is a little less intoxicating. Drink writer Robert Simonson went in search of Harvey and could find no record of him. The barman credited with creating the drink, Donato "Duke" Antone, was apparently living in Hartford, Connecticut, at the time—much too distant to be serving drunken Manhattan Beach surfers.

Whatever the actual origins of the cocktail, it became an icon of 1970s drinking culture, catapulting imports of Galliano up to 500,000 cases a year. It was the drink of the era. Even my parents, by no means heavy imbibers, kept a bottle at home. It's still there several decades later.

The drink that made Harvey a household name was a simple mix of vodka, orange juice, and Galliano—essentially a Screwdriver with a float of herbal liqueur. I've updated the drink for beer lovers, replacing flavorless vodka with refreshing hefeweizen. Though any wheat ale could work in this cocktail, my preference is for flavorful German classics such as Weihenstephaner, which bring more complexity to the party.

The flavors in this drink are a natural match: The anise and vanilla notes of Galliano go well with the orange juice, and the orange juice pairs naturally with wheat beer. Think of Belgian witbier with its addition of orange peel and coriander or the practice of serving a wedge of orange with American hefeweizen.

If purists scoff at the practice of putting orange wedges onto glasses of beer, then they'll call this drink pure heresy. I just call it delicious. It's easy drinking and perfect for brunch.

HARVEY WEISSBANGER

1 oz. Galliano
L'Autentico

2 oz. (60 ml)
fresh orange
juice

6 oz. (180 ml)
wheat beer

Twist of
orange peel,
for garnish

In the order listed, pour the ingredients into an ice-filled collins glass. Stir gently, then garnish with the twist of orange peel.

Serves 1

YAKIMA SLING

1 1/2 oz. reposado tequila

3/4 oz. fresh grapefruit juice

2/3 oz. Cinnamon Syrup
(store bought or homemade;
see recipe below)

1/2 oz. fresh lime juice

2 to 3 oz. (60 to 90 ml) IPA

Twist of grapefruit peel,
for garnish

Combine the tequila, grapefruit juice, syrup, and lime juice in a cocktail shaker. Shake with ice and strain into an ice-filled collins glass. Top with the IPA, stir to combine, and garnish with the grapefruit peel.

Serves 1

CINNAMON SYRUP

1 cup (200 g) sugar

1 cup (240 ml) water

4 cinnamon sticks, preferably
Ceylon cinnamon, broken

Combine the sugar, water, and cinnamon in a pot and bring to a boil, stirring to dissolve the sugar. Reduce the heat to maintain a simmer and simmer for about 5 minutes. Remove the pot from the heat and let the syrup cool, then strain and store it in a sealed glass bottle in the refrigerator. It will keep for a few weeks.

Makes about 1 1/2 cups (360 ml)

The Paloma, a favorite cocktail in Mexico and beyond, is traditionally made by mixing tequila with grapefruit soda. Whether prepared with commercial grapefruit soda or fresh ingredients, the cocktail is a testament to how well tequila and grapefruit go together. This recipe from Evan Martin, a bartender from Seattle, is a more complex take on that combination. The name *Yakima*, which appears here and in the Blushing Yakima (page 103), refers to the Yakima Valley, a region of Washington famous for growing hops.

Evan's Yakima Sling adds cinnamon syrup and the floral, hoppy bitterness of an IPA to the traditional Paloma. He uses the locally made Fremont Interurban IPA and intends this to be a "beer drinker's cocktail," appealing to the Pacific Northwest's love of IPAs with big, bitter flavors.

Use good tequila and a hoppy IPA for this cocktail. The cinnamon syrup can be bought commercially from B. G. Reynolds' or made at home.

The classic Boilermaker (page 42) has very little to do with mixology. Mixology, however, can have some fun with the Boilermaker. My friend Kevin Ludwig, proprietor of the award-winning Portland bar and restaurant Beaker and Flask until its closure in 2013, came up with the idea of dropping not just a shot of whiskey, but an entire whiskey cocktail, into a glass of beer. Kevin would make large batches of classic whiskey drinks, dividing them into shot glasses and chilling them in the freezer. Customers would drop one of these miniature cocktails into their beer, gradually flavoring the brew as they drank it down (or chugging it all at once, if they desired).

One of the standouts in Beaker and Flask's series of Boilermakers was the Vieux Carré. This mix of rye, cognac, sweet vermouth, Benedictine, and bitters is one of the iconic drinks of New Orleans. When visiting the French Quarter, it's worth making a trip to the rotating Carousel Bar at the Hotel Monteleone to enjoy one at its place of origin. But if making a Vieux Carré at home, consider dropping it into beer instead.

VIEUX CARRÉ BOILERMAKER

1 oz. Vieux Carré Mix,
see recipe below

12 to 16 oz. (360 to 480 ml) lager or pale ale

Pour the Vieux Carré mix into a shot glass. Pour the beer into a pint glass, allowing room for the shot glass that will soon be added. Drop the shot glass into the beer and enjoy.

Serves 1

VIEUX CARRÉ MIX

1 1/2 oz. rye whiskey

1 1/2 oz. cognac

1 1/2 oz. sweet vermouth

1/4 oz. Benedictine

4 dashes Angostura bitters

4 dashes Peychaud's bitters

Combine all the ingredients in a bottle, seal, and chill it in the freezer. The mixture will keep indefinitely.

Makes about 1/2 cup (120 ml)

Before the advent of refrigeration, hardworking Belgian farmers had a problem: They worked up quite a thirst during the summer harvest. These were the same months that were too hot for brewing beer; beer brewed in that weather was likely to ferment uncontrollably and spoil. The solution was saison, a beer brewed in the spring with enough hops and alcohol to last through the summer, yet light enough to be refreshing on a hot summer day.

Modern technology has freed brewing from the shackles of the seasons, but saison is still a fantastic beer to drink during the summer. Thankfully saisons, or "farmhouse ales" as they're often called, have caught on both as imports and as domestically produced craft beers. Usually golden in color, it's not uncommon for them to be accented with spices or given secondary fermentation in a corked bottle. It's a fantastic style to pair with food too. In his book *The Brewmaster's Table*, Brooklyn brewmaster Garret Oliver confesses that "if I were forced to choose one style to drink with every meal for the rest of my life, saison would have to be it."

Saison also finds its calling in refreshing beer cocktails. This one comes from the superbly talented bartender Karen Grill. Karen hails from New Jersey, enjoyed her first craft beer in Boston, and now tends bar at Sassafras Saloon in Los Angeles. She is equally at home with cocktails and beer, complementing her bar experience with a love for homebrewing.

This cocktail balances the bitter notes of the Italian aperitif Aperol with tart citrus, honey, and a pleasant herbal flavor from marjoram. Karen makes this with Smog City's LA Saison and notes that it can also work with a crisp pilsner.

BEER AND LOATHING

3/4 oz. Aperol

3/4 oz. fresh grapefruit juice

1/2 oz. fresh lemon juice

2 sprigs fresh marjoram,
plus 1 sprig for garnish

1/2 oz. Rich Honey Syrup,
see recipe below

3 to 4 oz. (90 to 120 ml) saison

Twist of grapefruit peel, for garnish

Combine the Aperol, citrus juices, 2 sprigs of the marjoram, and the syrup in a shaker with ice; shake and strain the liquid into an ice-filled collins glass. Top with a few ounces of saison and garnish with the remaining marjoram sprig and the grapefruit peel.

Serves 1

RICH HONEY SYRUP

1 1/2 cups (360 ml) honey

1/2 cup (120 ml) boiling water

In a small bowl, stir together the honey and boiling water until well combined. Let it cool, then store the syrup in a sealed bottle at room temperature. It will keep for a couple of weeks.

Makes about 1 3/4 cups (420 ml)

MAI TA-IPA

1 1/2 oz. IPA

1 oz. white rum

1 oz. aged rum

1 oz. fresh lime juice

3/4 oz. orgeat

1/2 oz. orange curaçao

Cocktail cherries, for garnish

Pour the beer, rums, lime juice, orgeat, and orange curaçao into a mixing glass and shake with ice. Strain the drink into an ice-filled rocks or collins glass. Garnish with cherries and a cocktail parasol.

Serves 1

Few cocktails have been as badly abused by time as Trader Vic's Mai Tai (although the Dry Martini could certainly make a claim). Vic's original recipe was a complex, rum-forward cocktail intended to highlight Wray & Nephew's seventeen-year-old aged rum with accents of lime, orange curaçao, and an almond syrup called orgeat. As tiki cocktail culture became more popular and spread more widely, the drink got dumbed down into a generic fruity rum concoction packed with sugar and arriving in frightening shades of neon.

A correctly prepared Mai Tai is a superbly balanced drink in an entirely different league than the excessively sweet impostors that often bear its name. And with the revival of classic cocktails in recent years, it's getting easier to find a good one. So how about we chance messing it up again by adding beer?

There's a motivation for this. Tiki drinks, though undeniably appealing, tend not to use many bitter elements. I've found that adding a splash of hoppy ale to tiki drinks can take them in an interesting direction, adding a touch of complexity. Shaking beer directly into cocktails also gives them a nice frothy head.

Ezra Johnson-Greenough and I served this twist on the Mai Tai at a Brewing Up Cocktails Spirited Dinner at the 2012 Tales of the Cocktail conference in New Orleans. We made it with Demerara rums from El Dorado, which have a full character that works great in this.

To add a little more funk, you could also try it with rhum agricole, which is distilled from fresh sugar cane juice, and a Jamaican rum like Smith & Cross. Just don't forget the cocktail parasol. You wouldn't want the cherries to catch a sunburn.

HOPPED UP NUI NUI

2 oz. (60 ml) aged rum

1 oz. IPA

½ oz. fresh lime juice

½ oz. fresh orange juice

¼ oz. Cinnamon Syrup,
page 86

¼ oz. Don's Spices #2

1 dash Angostura bitters

Cocktail cherry, for garnish

Fill a rocks glass with crushed ice. Combine all the ingredients in a shaker and shake them with ice, then strain the drink into the glass. Garnish with the cherry.

Serves 1

I ntellectual property among bartenders is a tricky thing. It's possible, though controversial, to trademark the name of a drink. Obtaining a patent is impractical. Copyright doesn't much apply to recipes or prevent competitors from recreating drinks. Once the recipe for a cocktail is made public, there's nothing a bartender can do to stop other people from making it.

Norms encourage those of us in the industry to give credit where due, and the Internet has made it easier than ever to track down the originators of various drinks. An ethos of openness and sharing has developed in the age of blogging, allowing new recipes and techniques to spread. Many bartenders publicize their creations in return for recognition and, perhaps, new customers.

It wasn't always this way. Bartenders can also be a secretive lot, hiding their recipes even from their own staff. Don the Beachcomber, one of the founding fathers of the tropical drink genre, went so far as to stock his bars with syrups enigmatically labeled only by number. His bartenders knew how much of each to pour into a cocktail, but didn't always know exactly what they were.

Credit for deciphering some of these goes to Jeff "Beachbum" Berry, a historian of tiki cocktail culture. For the Nui Nui, that meant identifying Don's "#2" and "#4."

By interviewing some of Don's former staff, he pieced together that the latter was simply a cinnamon syrup. The former remains shrouded in mystery; Jeff re-creates it as a flavorful mix of vanilla and allspice, which works well in the drinks that call for it. This combination is now known in tiki circles as Don's Spices #2.

The Nui Nui doesn't have the same name recognition as Trader Vic's Mai Tai, but it's one of my favorite tiki drinks. Just as in the Mai Ta-IPA (page 91), this beer cocktail variation uses a splash of hoppy ale to add a hint of bitterness to tropical spices.

Both cinnamon syrup and Don's Spices #2 are produced commercially by B. G. Reynolds' Syrups; I've also provided a recipe for homemade cinnamon syrup on page 86.

The White Collins is a contribution from Kristof Burm, a talented Belgian bartender I met on a trip making tea cocktails in Sri Lanka. He manages the bar at Josephine's in Antwerp, where he has featured several beer cocktails on the menu. When I contacted him asking for a cocktail using Belgian beer, he contributed this drink he created in collaboration with Marc Colfs, the Belgian brand ambassador for Bombay gins.

Belgian witbier gets its name from its white, hazy appearance. It also tends to accentuate its hops with other spices, notably coriander and sweet and bitter orange peels. It's an aromatic beer that's perfect for summer. In this riff on the Collins, the botanicals are accentuated even further with gin and a delicate licorice syrup.

Kristof makes this with Bombay Sapphire and garnishes it with a whole licorice root. The latter can be hard to find in the United States, so I've suggested a lemon peel as an alternative. For the beer, choose a good Belgian wit; Kristof recommends Steenbrugge Wit.

WHITE COLLINS

1 1/2 oz. gin

1 oz. fresh lemon juice

3/4 oz. Licorice Syrup,
see recipe below

3 to 4 oz. (90 to 120 ml) witbier

Licorice root or twist of lemon peel,
for garnish

Combine the gin, lemon juice, and syrup in a collins glass with ice. Stir, then top with the witbier. Stir again briefly to combine. Garnish with the licorice root or lemon peel.

Serves 1

LICORICE SYRUP

1 cup (200 g) sugar

1 tbsp. licorice root pieces

1 cup (240 ml) water

Combine the sugar, licorice, and water in a pot and bring to a simmer over medium heat. Immediately remove from the heat and let cool. Strain out the licorice pieces and store the syrup in a sealed glass bottle in the refrigerator. It will keep for several weeks.

Makes about 1 3/4 cups (420 ml)

PIÑA PICA

1 ½ oz. Serrano-Infused Mezcal, *see recipe below*

¾ oz. fresh lime juice

¾ oz. Easy Pineapple Shrub, *see recipe below*

½ oz. maraschino liqueur

3 to 4 oz. (90 to 120 ml) Mexican lager

Lime wheel, for garnish

Sal de gusano, for garnish

Combine the mezcal, lime juice, shrub, and maraschino liqueur in a shaker and shake with ice. Strain the drink into an ice-filled collins glass. Top with the lager, garnish with the lime wheel, and sprinkle a pinch of sal de gusano over the drink.

Serves 1

SERRANO-INFUSED MEZCAL

1 serrano chile, halved

500 ml mezcal (about 17 oz.)

Put the chile into the mezcal and allow it to infuse for 24 hours. Strain and bottle the infused mezcal. It will keep indefinitely.

Makes about 2 cups (500 ml)

EASY PINEAPPLE SHRUB

1 cup (240 ml) pineapple juice

1 cup (240 ml) apple cider vinegar

1 cup (200 g) sugar

Combine the ingredients in a bowl and stir until the sugar has dissolved. Bottle and refrigerate the shrub. It will keep for several weeks.

Makes about 2 ½ cups (600 ml)

This cocktail boasts the most adventurous garnish in the book: *sal de gusano*, translated literally as "worm salt." This Oaxacan condiment is actually made by mixing salt with dried chile peppers and *chinicuil*, worms that feed on agave plants. The worms are dried in the sun and toasted before being pounded into powder with the chiles and salt. Served with fresh fruit, *sal de gusano* lends a savory and spicy flavor to the mezcal drink.

Mezcal, too, can be an adventurous ingredient. It's a rustic agave spirit, the production of which is less rigidly defined than that of tequila. (Tequila is technically a specific type of mezcal, much like cognac is a type of brandy.) Until recently, most of the mezcal exported to the United States was very rough stuff, perhaps including a worm at the bottom of the bottle. It was the kind of thing you'd drink on a dare, not for pleasure.

That has changed, thankfully. Importers have introduced traditional mezcals of supremely high quality, elevating expectations for this wonderful spirit. Like single-malt Scotch, it's not necessarily the most approachable drink, but those who enjoy it can get quite passionate about it.

Dan Long features mezcal in this twist on the Michelada he served at Big Bar, a craft cocktail destination in the Los Feliz neighborhood of Los Angeles. Additional spice comes from an infusion of serrano pepper in mezcal, which is tempered with what Dan calls his "easy pineapple shrub"—a mix of pineapple juice, apple cider vinegar, and sugar that soothes the chile heat. A bit more depth and sweetness come from maraschino liqueur, lime juice provides acidity, and it's all finished off with easy-drinking Mexican lager.

Shrubs are a traditional method of preserving fruit juices with sugar and acidity, the latter typically provided by vinegar. Making shrubs was common practice before refrigeration, and today bartenders are reviving it for the delicious sweet-tart flavor shrubs can bring to a cocktail. Many recipes require heating on the stove or a cold process that can take days. Dan's Easy Pineapple Shrub requires neither and is simple and quick. Any shrub leftover over from making cocktails can be mixed with soda to make a refreshing nonalcoholic drink.

Preparing the ingredients for this drink takes a bit of time, but the effort of putting them together will be rewarded with one of the most refreshing cocktails in this book. And while the *sal de gusano* isn't strictly necessary, it's worth tracking down at a Latin market or online for the uniquely spicy and savory qualities it adds to the cocktail. A mixture of salt and ground chiles can work in its place.

HIBISCUS MICHELADA

Lime wedge, for garnish

Coarse salt, for the glass rim

1 1/2 oz. Hibiscus Syrup, *see recipe below*

3/4 oz. mezcal

3/4 oz. Agavero or other damiana liqueur

1/2 oz. fresh lime juice

1/2 tsp. habanero salsa, such as El Yucateco brand

6 oz. Mexican lager

Moisten the rim of a pint glass with the lime wedge and dip it in salt. Combine the syrup, mezcal, liqueur, lime juice, and hot sauce in the glass. Add ice, top with beer, and stir well. Garnish with the lime wedge.

Serves 1

HIBISCUS SYRUP

1/4 cup dried hibiscus

1 cup (240 ml) water

1 1/2 cups (300 g) sugar

Combine the hibiscus and water in a pot and bring to a boil. Remove from the heat, cover, and allow to steep for 20 minutes. Add the sugar and stir to dissolve, returning the pot to the heat if necessary. Strain out the hibiscus and store, refrigerated, in a clean glass bottle for up to 2 weeks.

Makes about 1 1/2 cups (360 ml)

As mentioned earlier in the book, the Michelada (page 41) is an infinitely variable recipe. The base of lager, lime, and spice is open to many complementary additions, especially when spirits are brought into play (also see pages 95–96). Micheladas featuring Mexican spirits now make frequent appearances on cocktail menus, offering a higher-proof take on classic versions of the drink.

When seeking a contemporary Michelada for this book, I turned to Mi Mero Mole, my favorite place for tacos in Portland. The menu at Mi Mero Mole focuses on *guisados* (homestyle stews) and stir-fries that are popular among urban diners in Mexico City. At the restaurant, owners Nick Zukin and Pablo Portilla offer these dishes alongside traditional Mexican beverages like *horchata* and *aqua de jamaica*, inventive cocktails, and one of the city's best selections of tequila and mezcal.

The key ingredient in Mi Mero Mole's riff on the Michelada is a syrup made by steeping hibiscus flowers in hot water. Combined with Agavero, a tequila-based damiana flower liqueur, it gives the cocktail a vibrant red color and a floral sweetness that pairs well with fruity habanero salsa. A small pour of assertive mezcal and a squeeze of lime balance the sweetness of the other ingredients.

FIRECRACKER

1 1/2 oz. rye whiskey

3/4 oz. Aperol

1/2 oz. fresh lemon juice

1/2 oz. Rich Simple Syrup, *see recipe below*

2 dashes orange bitters

4 to 5 oz. (120 to 150 ml) hefeweizen

Lemon peel, for garnish

Combine the rye, Aperol, lemon juice, syrup, and bitters in a shaker and shake with ice. Strain the drink into an ice-filled pint glass. Top it with the hefeweizen and garnish with the lemon peel.

Serves 1

RICH SIMPLE SYRUP

1 cup (200 g) sugar

1/2 cup (120 ml) water

Combine the sugar and water in a pot and heat, stirring, until the sugar has dissolved. Store the syrup in a sealed bottle in the refrigerator. It will keep for several weeks.

Makes about 1 cup (240 ml)

Fans of whiskey-based cocktails will enjoy this one from Portland bartender Lauren Scott. Lauren created this for Spirit of 77, a Portland sports bar named for the year when the Portland Trailblazers won the NBA championship. Featuring craft beer, quality cocktails, a lofty ceiling, and free pop-a-shot basketball, Spirit of 77 is a Portland take on the sports bar, with better drinks than one normally expects to find in similar venues. She has since moved on to the new Portland bar Angel Face.

Aperol, an Italian digestif with bitter orange flavors, goes particularly well with the hefeweizen in this cocktail. The spicy note of rye whiskey comes through nicely too. The combination is both strong and refreshing. Lauren makes the Firecracker with Jim Beam rye and Ayinger Bräu-Weisse for the beer, which she likes for its banana aroma. Feel free to make it with a different rye or German hefeweizen. (The rich simple syrup used here is a syrup with a higher concentration of sugar than ordinary simple syrup, giving it a richer body.)

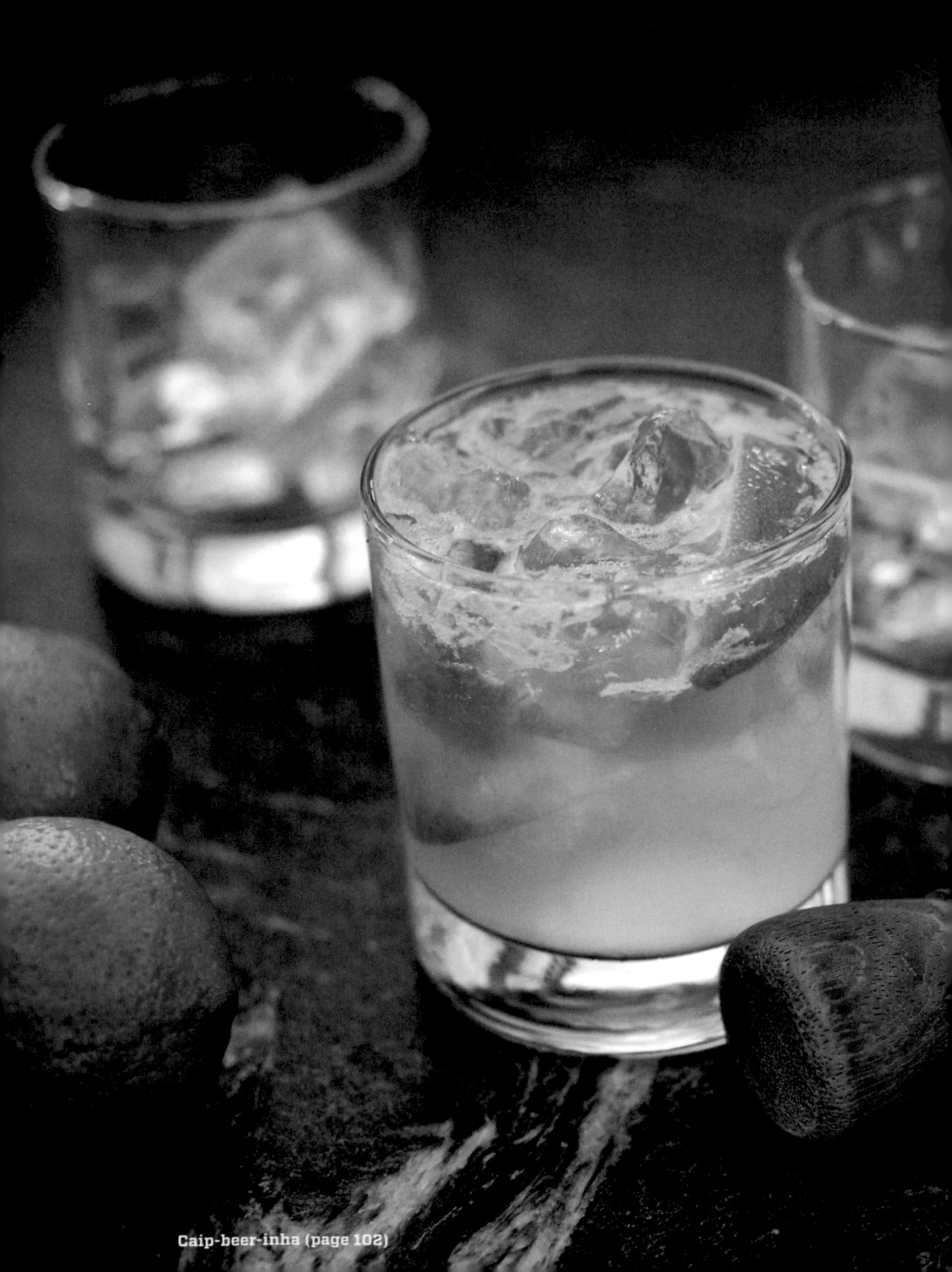

Caip-beer-inha (page 102)

CAIP-BEER-INHA

½ lime, cut lengthwise, quartered, and trimmed of pith

1 tbsp. superfine sugar

2 oz. (60 ml) cachaça

1 oz. IPA

Muddle the lime and sugar in a shaker until the sugar is mostly dissolved in the juice from the lime (using superfine sugar will make this easier). Add the cachaça. Add ice and shake. Pour the contents of the shaker, without straining, into a rocks glass. Float the IPA on top and serve.

Serves 1

One of the most popular cocktails in the world was little known until recently in the United States. Named the national drink of Brazil, it marries Brazilian cachaça—a spirit with similarities to rum but distilled exclusively from sugar cane juice rather than molasses—with muddled limes and sugar. The drink's popularity drives the consumption of more than a billion liters of cachaça each year, almost all of it in Brazil. (Germany, interestingly, makes up the second biggest market for the spirit, where it is so popular that Caipirinhas are sometimes served hot in the winter. A strange idea, but it works.)

My collaborator, Ezra Johnson-Greenough, came up with the idea of making a Caipirinha with IPA for a party celebrating the second anniversary of our Brewing Up Cocktails series of events. Much like in the Mai Ta-IPA (page 91) and Hopped Up Nui Nui (page 92), the IPA here adds just a touch of bitterness. Use a light hand with the beer, as too much of it can overpower the other flavors.

This is an updated version of our original Caip-beer-inha. The limited number of ingredients in this drink puts the focus on the spirit, so it's important to use a good cachaça. Industrial brands are hot, boring, and have little to recommend them except their low price. Higher-quality cachaça is complex and carries the grassy notes of fresh sugar cane. There's a world of difference between the cheap stuff and the real thing.

I make this drink with Novo Fogo Silver, which opened my eyes to the possibilities of cachaça a few years ago and for whom I now organize cocktail events across the country.

ragos Axinte, the entrepreneur behind Novo Fogo cachaça, took the idea of a Caip-beer-inha and ran with it, creating multiple variations of the cocktail.

He realized that the combination of cachaça, citrus, beer, and syrup or liqueur held untapped potential as a formula for creating new drinks. He matches the tones of the ingredients, as in this drink that pairs darker barrel-aged cachaça with amaretto and brown ale. Its rounded, nutty flavors make it a perfect cocktail for autumn.

There are only a few barrel-aged cachaças in the United States; they are more common in Brazil, especially in the south. Novo Fogo Barrel-Aged Cachaça spends two years in used bourbon barrels and works very nicely in this cocktail.

Many good brown ales are available with wide distribution, such as Sierra Nevada Tumbler, Uinta Bristlecone, and Smuttynose Old Brown Dog. Dragos also recommends Xingu Black Beer, a dark lager from Brazil, for a more fully Brazilian take on the drink. For the fruit, use high-quality preserved maraschino, morello, or similar cherries.

BLUSHING YAKIMA

3 preserved cherries

2 oz. (60 ml) aged cachaça

1 1/2 oz. brown ale

1 oz. fresh lime juice

1/2 oz. amaretto liqueur

1/2 oz. Simple Syrup, *see recipe below*

Muddle the cherries in the bottom of a shaker glass or tin. Add the remaining ingredients, along with ice, then shake them hard. Pour the contents of the shaker, without straining, into a rocks glass and serve.

Serves 1

SIMPLE SYRUP

1 cup (200 g) sugar

1 cup (240 ml) water

Combine the sugar and water in a pot and heat, stirring, over medium heat until the sugar has fully dissolved. Store the syrup in a sealed bottle in the refrigerator. It will keep for several weeks.

Makes 1 1/2 cups (360 ml)

When I moved to Portland in 2008, the local cocktail mecca was the swanky Teardrop Lounge in the Pearl District. Displayed on Teardrop's stylish circular bar were rows of blue glass dropper bottles filled with various housemade bitters and tinctures.

Five years later, high-quality craft cocktails have diffused throughout the city, and patrons seeking a good drink could be just about anywhere. Teardrop, though, remains at the top of its game, serving a three-page menu of original creations, classic drinks, and contributions from friends all over the world.

Teardrop has featured several beer cocktails on its menu over the years. When I asked owner Daniel Shoemaker to submit one for this book, he chose this one above all the others. It makes creative use of fruity Belgian kriek—a tart lambic beer flavored with cherries—by reducing it with spices. This is an ideal technique for home use or for bars without tap beer, as the reduction will keep for several weeks in the refrigerator, ensuring that beer doesn't go to waste.

The Strange Bedfellows manages to combine spirits, wine, and beer in one ambrosial cocktail. It's a complex riff on a Manhattan, with the lambic reduction and ice wine standing in for sweet vermouth. The apple brandy and allspice dram round it out with fall flavors. For the brandy, I'd suggest the "bottled in bond" 100-proof apple brandy from Laird's. If, unlike Teardrop, one doesn't have a dropper bottle of allspice dram, just be sure to use a similarly tiny amount. A little of this goes a long way.

Traditional Belgian lambics are dry, sour, expensive, and exquisite. Those are not the bottles to reach for here. The sweeter, more widely available Lindemans Kriek is what Daniel uses to make his reduction, and its higher sugar content and lower price make it the perfect choice for this application.

STRANGE BEDFELLOWS

1 1/2 oz. rye whiskey

1 oz. Kriek Lambic Reduction, *see recipe below*

3/4 oz. vin de glace (ice wine)

1/2 oz. applejack or apple brandy

8 drops allspice dram

Cocktail cherry, for garnish

In a mixing glass, stir together all the ingredients with ice and strain into a chilled cocktail glass. Garnish with the cherry.

Serves 1

KRIEK LAMBIC REDUCTION

2 (12-oz./360-ml) bottles or 1 (25-oz./750-ml) bottle kriek

2 lemons, thinly sliced

1/4 cup (30 g) rose hips

1/2 vanilla bean, split lengthwise

Pour the kriek into a pot. Add the remaining ingredients and simmer over low to medium heat until reduced by about one-third. Let the reduction cool to room temperature, strain, and store it in a sterilized glass bottle (see page 23) in the refrigerator. It will keep for a couple of weeks.

Makes about 1 cup (240 ml)

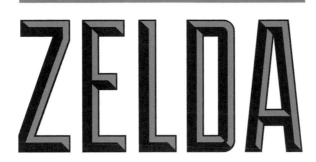

ZELDA

1 egg white

2 oz. (60 ml) gin, preferably Small's

3/4 oz. fresh lime juice

3/4 oz. Kriek Syrup, *see recipe below*

Raspberries, for garnish

Combine the ingredients in a shaker and shake without ice to aerate the egg white. Add ice and shake again. Strain the drink into a chilled cocktail glass and garnish with the raspberries.

Serves 1

KRIEK SYRUP

1 cup (240 ml) Kriek Lambic Reduction, *see page 104*

1 cup (200 g) sugar

Combine the kriek reduction and sugar in a pot and heat, stirring, until the sugar has dissolved. Store the syrup in a sealed bottle in the refrigerator. It will keep for several weeks.

Makes about 1 3/4 cups (420 ml)

Beer cocktails and pink drinks: Who says they're mutually exclusive? The Zelda gets its rosy hue from a syrup made with the kriek reduction used to make Strange Bedfellows (page 104). I sought additional ways to use the reduction, and found that mixing it with an equal volume of sugar made a tart, flavorful, and vibrantly colored ingredient for cocktails. It's sort of like making a grenadine out of beer.

This drink is a straightforward spin on a classic Clover Club, with the sweetness coming from the kriek syrup. Shaking it with egg white gives it a soft texture that makes it dangerously easy to drink.

I generally avoid specifying brands of spirits in this book, but I make an exception in this case for the Oregon-made Small's Gin from Ransom Spirits. Distilled with raspberries and cardamom among its botanicals, it has fruit and spice notes that can be difficult to work with in some gin cocktails. In the right drink, however, it sings. This is the right drink. Other gins will do satisfactorily too, but if Small's is available I highly recommend using it.

RAMBLE ON

1 1/2 oz. rye whiskey

1/2 oz. fresh lemon juice

1/2 oz. Amaro Nonino

1 heaping bar spoon Raspberry Lambic Jam, *see recipe below*

1 cracked cardamom pod

1 sprig fresh mint

Combine the rye, lemon juice, Amaro Nonino, and jam in a shaker with ice. Shake, then pour, without straining, into a rocks glass. Garnish with the cardamom pod and mint.

Serves 1

RASPBERRY LAMBIC JAM

1 (25-oz./750-ml) bottle framboise lambic

10 oz. (280 g) raspberries

1 3/4 cups (350 g) sugar, preferably superfine

1/4 cup (30 g) dry pectin

3/4 oz. fresh lemon juice

Peel of 1/2 orange

1/2 oz. Cardamom Tincture, *see recipe below*

Pour the lambic into a large, wide pan and stir it periodically for about 20 minutes, to allow the gas to dissipate. Add the raspberries and blend them with an immersion blender to a puree. Place the pan over medium heat and bring it to a simmer, then add the sugar, pectin, lemon juice, and orange peel. Allow the mixture to simmer until it has reduced to about 1 1/2 cups (360 ml), keeping an eye on it to make sure it does not boil over. Remove the orange peel and add the cardamom tincture. Pour the jam into a sterilized glass jar (see page 23) and refrigerate. If the jam hasn't set after 24 hours, return it to the stovetop to reduce slightly more. Stored in the sealed jar in the refrigerator, it will keep for a couple of weeks, or indefinitely, if processed using standard canning techniques.

Makes about 1 1/2 cups (340 ml)

CARDAMOM TINCTURE

2 oz. (60 ml) vodka

12 cracked green cardamom pods

Combine the vodka and cardamom in a sealed glass container and set them aside to infuse at room temperature for 5 days. Strain and bottle. Stored at room temperature, the tincture will keep indefinitely.

Makes 2 ounces (60 ml)

The sweet, fruity style of lambic beers made by Lindemans is a favorite ingredient of bartenders. This makes sense. They're approachable and flavorful, with a high sugar content that makes them easy to transform into cocktail ingredients. They're also much cheaper than traditional lambic beers, which are made with spontaneous fermentation, frequently blended from beers that have been aged, and often carbonated via a secondary fermentation in the bottle. These are wonderful, bracing beers, and they can be quite expensive. They're so fantastic on their own, even I would be reluctant to mix them into a cocktail.

However, as the recipes in this book attest, I have no qualms about mixing with the more affordable Belgian fruit beers. In the Strange Bedfellows (page 104) and Zelda (page 107), they are reduced and made into syrups, respectively. In this drink, Austin bartender Jason Stevens of Bar Congress takes raspberry lambic and turns it into jam. Shaken with rye whiskey, citrus, and the bittersweet Italian liqueur Amaro Nonino, it makes a lightly fruity cocktail that expertly balances the rye with sweeter ingredients.

Of all the amari called for in this book, Nonino is one of the most complex and one of the most approachable. Made by infusing herbs in grape distillate and aging in barrels, it has a softer edge than many other bitter liqueurs. I was happy that Jason contributed this recipe if for no other reason than to provide an excuse for me to finally buy a bottle; it's great on the rocks or served as an after-dinner digestif.

For truly dedicated drinkers, the Nonino family also sells their amaro in imperial-sized 6.3-liter bottles that come with a glass pipette for drawing out the spirit. It's not in American liquor stores, so we'll have to content ourselves with the more sensibly sized 750-ml bottles.

Making this cocktail requires a bit more culinary skill than others in the book. Fortunately, making jam is pretty straightforward. A good way to test if it is ready to be removed from the heat: Chill a plate in the freezer. Spoon a little of the hot liquid onto the chilled plate, and if it thickens within a minute, it's ready to be canned and chilled. Check online for the USDA's *Complete Guide to Home Canning*, which can be downloaded for free.

In addition to its uses behind the bar, the raspberry lambic jam is nice to have on hand. It pairs well with goat cheese; try it with Humboldt Fog and a good, crisp cracker.

VANDAAG GIN COCKTAIL

1 dash Kirschwasser-Absinthe Mix, *see recipe below*

2 oz. (60 ml) genever

1 1/2 tsp. Rauchbier Syrup, *see recipe below*

2 dashes grapefruit bitters

1 dash Angostura bitters

Twist of lemon peel, for garnish

Rinse a rocks glass with the Kirschwasser-Absinthe Mix, discarding excess. Combine the remaining ingredients in a mixing glass and stir them with ice. Strain the drink into the rocks glass over ice or one large cube. Garnish with the lemon peel.

Serves 1

KIRSCHWASSER-ABSINTHE MIX

1 oz. kirschwasser

1 oz. absinthe

Mix the kirschwasser and absinthe together and pour them into a bottle, such as a clean bitters bottle with a dasher top. It will keep indefinitely at room temperature.

Makes 2 ounces (60 ml)

RAUCHBIER SYRUP

4 oz. (120 ml) rauchbier

1 cup (200 g) cane sugar

Pour the beer into a pot, stirring it and allowing it to de-gas for 20 minutes to help prevent it from spilling over when heated. Add the sugar and heat, stirring, until the sugar has dissolved and the mixture is combined. Pour the syrup into a bottle, seal, and refrigerate. It will keep for a couple of weeks.

Makes about 10 ounces (300 ml)

I never had the opportunity to visit Vandaag, a Dutch bar and restaurant that operated in New York from 2010 to 2012. I wish that I had, because their drink menu focused on three of my favorite things: genever, aquavit, and beer cocktails.

Bar manager Katie Stipe put their signature Vandaag Gin Cocktail at the top of the list. This was her twist on the Improved Holland Gin Cocktail, a vintage descendant of the Old Fashioned that accents Dutch genever with a hint of absinthe. Instead of using sugar, Katie sweetened the drink with rich beer syrups, varying the selection with the seasons: stout in winter, spring bock in spring, and saison in summer. In the fall, Vandaag served the version included here, employing a syrup made with rauchbier, an intensely smoky German-style beer.

The smokiness of rauchbier comes from drying the malt over an open flame, which imparts flavor to the barley grains. The process is similar to that which gives peaty Scotches their distinctive taste; fans of Islay Scotches will find much to like in rauchbier. Aecht Schlenkerla from Bamberg is the brand most commonly found in the United States.

As Katie notes, some of the beers she used were a bit pricey to be mixing into cocktails, such as the Emelisse Rauchbier she chose for this one. Incorporating them into syrups that could be used a teaspoon or two at a time made them financially practical for bar use. At home, beer syrups are a unique way of sweetening and flavoring cocktails. I suggest using just enough beer to make the desired quantity of syrup and imbibing the remainder. The recipe here makes about 10 ounces (300 ml) and can be easily scaled up or down, keeping the proportions intact.

Until a few years ago, genever was often difficult to find on the American market. Today it's much easier, thanks to the relaunch of Bols Genever, which I worked on for several years. There remains some confusion about the labeling of genever. It's made in both *jonge* and *oude* styles, which, as one would expect, do translate as "young" and "old." This has nothing to do with barrel aging, however; the terms refer to the style of production.

Jonge genever is made in a more modern style, with less of the whiskeylike distillate (called malt wine) that forms the heart of traditional genever. Oude genever is made in the old style, with much more maltiness. It can be bought aged or unaged. The assertive flavor of oude genever can take some getting used to, but it's the type to reach for in drinks like this one.

At Vandaag, they served their Gin Cocktail with the unaged Bols Genever, which has maltiness in spades. For a slightly milder version of the drink, try the barrel-aged genever that Bols recently introduced.

WIT-TY FLIP

1 1/2 oz. Drambuie

3/4 oz. fresh lemon juice

2 dashes orange bitters

2 dashes allspice dram

1 large egg

4 oz. (120 ml) witbier

Freshly grated nutmeg, for garnish

Combine the Drambuie, lemon juice, bitters, allspice dram, and egg in a cocktail glass and shake them hard with ice. Pour the beer into a chalice or pilsner glass. Strain the shaken cocktail into the beer and garnish it with freshly grated nutmeg.

Serves 1

Flips, whether served hot or cold, are usually thought of as winter drinks. I set out specifically to make this version as a summer flip, lightening the heavy body with four ounces of effervescent Belgian-style witbier. Brewed with wheat and often flavored with coriander and orange peel, it pairs wonderfully with citrus, spice, and orange bitters.

The inspiration for this cocktail is the Duke, a fairly esoteric drink that's topped with a float of Champagne. It appears in *The Cafe Royal Cocktail Book*, a compilation of recipes published by the United Kingdom Bartenders' Guild in 1937. I've had a soft spot for the drink ever since first trying it in 2008. Its main ingredient, the Scotch-based herbal liqueur Drambuie, is more often used as an accent to cocktails than as a base spirit. I liked that the Duke inverted this practice, putting the Drambuie front and center. It was a drink ripe for adaptation to a beer cocktail, and when I presented this at a Drambuie cocktail competition a few years ago, it won second place.

Instead of shaking the beer into the cocktail, it's poured into the glass ahead of the other ingredients. Pouring the heavier ingredients into the lighter beer ensures that everything mixes thoroughly.

BEER NOG

4 large eggs

1 1/2 cups (360 ml) whole milk

1 cup (240 ml) heavy cream

8 oz. (240 ml) porter

4 oz. (120 ml) cognac

1/2 cup (100 g) sugar

2 dashes freshly grated nutmeg

1 vanilla bean, split

Whisk the eggs in a bowl, then add the remaining ingredients and whisk to thoroughly combine them. If serving the nog fresh, slip in an ice block or serve it in glasses with large cubes.

If storing, seal the nog in a sterilized glass bottle (see page 23) and keep it refrigerated. Discard the Beer Nog if it bubbles, undergoes sudden changes in appearance, or smells in any way suspect.

Serves 5 or 6

At Rob Roy in Seattle, the traditional Advent calendar gets a spirituous boost with twenty-five days of holiday cocktails. For each day leading up to Christmas, Anu Apte, owner of the swank Belltown cocktail lounge, offers a different seasonal cocktail. Loyal customers who fill up their advent cards are treated to free drinks in the new year.

Few drinks are as emblematic of holiday cheer as eggnog. Rob Roy's Beer Nog is a twist on the traditional recipe that adds a healthy serving of porter. The malty, roasty notes of the beer complement Christmas spices and the creaminess of the nog very well. A batch of this nog is perfect for entertaining beer and cocktail lovers alike at a holiday party.

This Beer Nog is absolutely delicious fresh, but it can be aged too. Aging egg-based drinks may seem like an odd idea, but aging eggnog is a tradition with a long history. The ingredients in the drink mellow and marry their flavors together over time. I've enjoyed very tasty eggnogs aged for several years. At Rob Roy, they keep this one in small oak barrels. At home, one can store it refrigerated in a sterilized, sealed glass bottle. Whether to serve it fresh or aged is a matter of personal preference.

If serving this fresh, I suggest either spooning out some of the inside of the vanilla bean and adding it to the mixture, or applying some force with the whisk to ensure that the vanilla flavor fully infuses the nog.

Hanging above the bar at the Dead Rabbit in New York City are three engraved glass plates. These are trophies from the 2013 Tales of the Cocktail conference, where bar manager Jack McGarry and his crew took home the awards for World's Best New Bar, World's Best Cocktail Menu, and International Bartender of the Year. These are major accomplishments, and while sitting at the Dead Rabbit bar and perusing the menu of seventy-two cocktails, it becomes apparent that the honors are deserved.

An entire page of the menu is devoted to beer cocktails inspired by vintage recipes, often taking significant departures from the originals to update them for the modern palate. A fantastic example of this is Jack's Porterberry, inspired by Aleberry, an old-fashioned warm ale drink thickened with oatmeal. Jack liked the idea of using other ingredients to give a beer cocktail body and contemplated others that might work. The result is this fliplike concoction that uses butter instead of oats, is served cold, and makes use of the wide variety of spirits at a modern bar's disposal.

This drink calls for a lot of ingredients, but only one of them—the Italian herbal liqueur Strega—requires a particular brand. The Scotch should be a peaty one, probably from Islay. Choose an English-style rum with some character and a robust porter. For the vanilla syrup, I'd suggest the commercially available B. G. Reynolds'. To make it exactly as they do at the Dead Rabbit, use Bowmore 12 for the Scotch, Pusser's for the rum, and American Founders Porter for the beer. The Dead Rabbit even uses their own house Orinoco bitters, available for sale on their website; Angostura bitters will also work just fine.

This is an excellent cocktail, but be aware that it does pack a serious punch. With nearly 4 ounces (120 ml) of booze and a bit of beer, too, it's the kind of drink that can sneak up on you.

PORTERBERRY

1 ½ oz. peaty Scotch

1 ½ oz. English-style rum

1 ½ oz. porter

¾ oz. fresh lemon juice

½ oz. Strega

½ oz. vanilla syrup

1 tsp. soft butter

2 dashes Orinoco or Angostura bitters

Freshly grated nutmeg, for garnish

Lemon peel

Combine all the ingredients except the nutmeg and lemon peel in a cocktail shaker with ice, shake hard, and strain into a wineglass, large cocktail glass, or other suitable vessel. Grate the nutmeg over the surface of the drink. Express the lemon peel over the drink for aromatics and discard the peel.

Serves 1

HOOPS AND GARTERS

1 1/2 oz. Averna

3/4 oz. Simple Syrup, *see page 103*

3/4 oz. fresh lemon juice

1/2 oz. fresh orange juice

3 dashes Cinnamon-Infused Angostura Bitters, *see recipe below*

3 to 4 oz. (90 to 120 ml) pilsner

Twist of orange peel, for garnish

Shake the Averna, syrup, citrus juices, and bitters in a shaker with ice. Strain into an ice-filled collins glass. Top with a few ounces of the pilsner and stir lightly to combine. Garnish with the twist of orange peel.

Serves 1

CINNAMON-INFUSED ANGOSTURA BITTERS

1 (4-oz./120-ml) bottle Angostura bitters

2 cinnamon sticks, about 2 in. (5 cm) long

Combine the bitters and cinnamon sticks in a clean glass jar. Seal and allow them to infuse for 7 to 10 days. Remove the cinnamon and pour the bitters back into the original bottle. It will keep indefinitely at room temperature.

Makes about 4 ounces (120 ml)

Averna appears in two drinks in this book, and the drinks could not be more different from each other. My Averna Stout Flip (page 149) is rich, dark, and creamy. This one, from my friend Benjamin "Banjo" Amberg at the Portland bar Clyde Common, is crisp and effervescent with an underlying depth and sweetness.

Banjo's inspiration for this was a different beer cocktail, the recipe for which he thought sounded awful. Making it confirmed his suspicion, but also led him to create a great drink. "I rinsed my mouth out with a glass of whiskey, cursed the creator, and decided I was going to make a similar drink, but, you know, palatable." At that he succeeded, and the drink soon made it onto the Clyde Common menu with a name that alludes to "Being for the Benefit of Mr. Kite" from the Beatles' *Sgt. Pepper's Lonely Hearts Club Band* album.

One could conceivably make the drink with regular Angostura bitters, but the cinnamon-infused bitters really are a nice touch. They're easy to make and handy to have around for adding spice to cocktails that call for aromatic bitters, such as an Old Fashioned or a Manhattan.

So far in this book, fruity Belgian lambic beers have been transformed into a reduction, a syrup, and even a jam. In this cocktail, finally, the beer is used as-is, topping the cocktail straight from the bottle or tap.

The star of this cocktail—from Tacy Rowland of Bōl in Vail, Colorado—is Campari, the bright red, bittersweet aperitif from Italy. Campari and orange juice is a classic pairing that works very well here. A splash of Scotch—Tacy suggests the excellent Auchentoshan 12 year—adds a little more depth, and the hopped grapefruit bitters are a fitting touch for a beer cocktail.

The framboise lambic helps take the edge off, but this is still an assertively bitter drink that allows the flavor of Campari to shine through. Fans of cocktails like the Negroni, Boulevardier, or Americano will surely enjoy this one; Tacy originally made it for a cocktail competition in Austin, Texas, sponsored by Campari, where it took first place.

SUMMIT SUNRISE

1 1/2 oz. Campari

1 oz. fresh orange juice

1/2 oz. Scotch

3 dashes Bittermens Hopped Grapefruit Bitters

2 oz. (60 ml) framboise lambic

Twist of grapefruit peel, for garnish

Twist of orange peel, for garnish

Combine the Campari, orange juice, Scotch, and bitters in a cocktail shaker and shake with ice. Strain the drink into a rocks glass over a large ice cube and top with the lambic. Garnish with the twists of grapefruit and orange peel.

Serves 1

Abbey Street Punch (page 124)

ABBEY STREET PUNCH

8 oz. (240 ml)
Irish whiskey

8 oz. (240 ml)
Irish stout

8 oz. (240 ml)
club soda

6 oz. (180 ml)
fresh lemon
juice

6 oz. (180 ml)
Simple Syrup,
see page 103

4 oz. (120 ml)
Jamaican rum

2 oz. (60 ml)
allspice dram

Freshly grated
nutmeg,
for garnish

Lime wheels,
for garnish

Combine all the ingredients in a punch bowl with 1 cup (240 ml) crushed ice, then slip in a large block of ice. Grate nutmeg over the surface of the punch. Ladle punch into individual glasses garnished with the lime wheels.

Serves 6 to 8

a very pleasant flavor" to Uncle Toby Punch, a very similar recipe from his *Bar-Tender's Guide* of 1862 that mixed the beer with brandy and rum.

The Abbey Street Punch from Polite Provisions, a fantastic bar in San Diego run by accomplished bartender Erick Castro, combines this technique with a contemporary approach to mixology, melding Irish beer and whiskey with Jamaican rum and allspice dram. It's a terrific punch for parties and can be easily scaled upward for larger groups.

At Polite Provisions, Erick makes this with Jameson Irish Whiskey, Guinness stout, and Appleton V/X rum. The Appleton isn't as assertively funky as the Smith & Cross pot-still rum called for elsewhere in this book, but it still has some of that distinctive Jamaican flavor. It's also very affordably priced, making it an excellent choice for large bowls of punch.

A dding dark beer to smooth out spirit-forward punch is a trick with a long history. For instance, there's the Blow My Skull (page 39) from Chapter 1, which uses porter to soften the blow of strong Jamaican rum. Jerry Thomas mentioned the practice too, noting that "porter gives a richness, and to some ter gives a richness, and to some

I n my home state of Texas, one of the popular drinks is the Beer Rita: a giant glass of frozen Margarita slush with an upturned bottle of Mexican lager sticking out of it. While these may not be made with the highest-quality ingredients, I understand the appeal in the high heat and humidity of a Texas summer, and there's no denying that beer and agave spirits have an affinity for each other.

This is a more refined take on the same combination from Denver, Colorado, bartender Ryan Conklin. Ryan is one of the city's most knowledgeable bartenders when it comes to beer, and is one of the few talented mixologists who is also certified as a Cicerone (the beer world's equivalent to a sommelier). When I met him, he was running the impressive beer program at Euclid Hall, where he frequently featured beer cocktails on the menu.

The name of this cocktail alludes to the tequila and beer Ryan uses: Siete Leguas blanco tequila and Tank 7 farmhouse ale from Boulevard Brewing. One can experiment with other tequilas—although Siete Leguas is fantastic—and with other farmhouse ales. But be aware that at 8.5 percent alcohol, the Tank 7 weighs in a bit heavier than the average farmhouse ale, which seems to work in the drink's favor.

SIETE Y SIETE

1 oz. blanco tequila

1/4 oz. agave nectar

1/4 oz. fresh lime juice

8 oz. farmhouse ale or saison

Lime wheel, for garnish

Combine the tequila, agave nectar, and lime juice in a tulip glass, then top with the beer. Stir gently to combine, then garnish with the lime wheel.

Serves 1

KOOEY KOOEY KOOEY

2 oz. (60 ml)
coconut porter

1 ½ oz.
coconut milk

1 ½ oz. aged
rum

½ oz. coffee
liqueur

½ oz.
allspice dram

Angostura
bitters,
for garnish

Combine the porter, coconut milk, rum, coffee liqueur, and allspice dram in a shaker. Shake them with ice, then strain the drink into a wineglass or similarly sized vessel. Garnish with the Angostura bitters on the surface of the drink, either dashed on top or sprayed from a misting bottle.

Serves 1

This is a drink that Ezra Johnson-Greenough, Yetta Vorobik, and I created for the second anniversary party of our Brewing Up Cocktails series of events. Hosting outdoors in the middle of July, we rented a portable bamboo bar, donned Hawaiian shirts, and set up shop in the backyard of the Hop and Vine. All of our drinks for that menu—which was presented in the jaws of a spit-roasted pig—had a tropical component, combining beer with tiki-style cocktails.

Ezra came up with the brilliant idea of combining coconut milk with coconut porter, creating a drink that had the creaminess of a flip without using any eggs or dairy. The result is this cocktail that straddles the line between festive party drink and rich dessert. (The silly name, by the way, is an allusion to old Justice League International comic books. It seemed like a good idea at the time.)

The rum in this should be of the dark English variety; English Harbour was our go-to choice, and I've also had good results with El Dorado 8 year. For the coffee liqueur, I like Galliano Ristretto, which has a more bittersweet flavor than most. The most widely available coconut porter comes from Maui Brewing Company in Hawaii, which accents dark malt with toasted coconut flavor and works wonderfully in this drink. In a pinch, a quality stout or porter can make a good stand-in.

A few years ago, my hometown of Houston, Texas, was not a city known for its cocktail or beer cultures. That's rapidly changing, thanks in large part to entrepreneur Bobby Heugel, who co-owns Houston's premier cocktail lounge, Anvil Bar and Refuge, and the beer mecca the Hay Merchant. He and his staff have done an amazing job elevating expectations for new cocktail and beer bars in the city, so it's no surprise that beer cocktails occasionally pop up on the Anvil menu.

This drink comes courtesy of Anvil bartender Kenneth Freeman. It evolved from his attempts to create a cocktail with Punch alla Fiamma, an unusual liqueur produced by the Italian distillery Varnelli.

Although it's a quality spirit, it's the sort of strange liquor that can linger on the bar unused until the right cocktail is found for it. My own bottle had been sitting on the shelf until I came across Kenneth's drink on a visit home.

Kenneth's goal was to create something refreshing and easy-drinking with the Punch. He pairs its rich, herbaceous, and citrusy sweetness with nutty orgeat, gin, and lemon.

Finally, he rounds out the cocktail with the maltiness of a good Scotch ale. "Only when I tried this," he says, "did the drink truly come to life."

A "shim" is a term for a low-proof cocktail coined by writer Dinah Sanders, and the "twice-told" in the name refers to this being the second iteration of this cocktail that Kenneth came up with. The Anvil recipe calls for making this with Beefeater gin and Oskar Blues Old Chub Scotch ale, both of which work very well. Other London dry gins can also be used in this drink, and I've made it with Great Divide's Claymore Scotch Ale to good effect too.

TWICE-TOLD SHIM

1/2 oz. gin

1/2 oz. Punch alla Fiamma

1/2 oz. orgeat

1/2 oz. fresh lemon juice

1/4 oz. Rich Simple Syrup, *see page 98*

1 oz. Scotch ale

Lemon wheel, for serving

1/2 fresh strawberry, for garnish

Combine the gin, Punch, orgeat, lemon juice, and simple syrup in a shaker. Shake with ice, then add the Scotch ale. Strain the drink into a rocks glass filled with crushed ice. Garnish with the lemon wheel and half strawberry.

Serves 1

Allison Webber is one of an increasing number of talented bartenders Oregon has lost to sunny California. She created this cocktail for a competition in Portland, where it took second place to a creation from Scotch expert and talented mixologist Tommy Klus. Being beaten by Tommy in cocktail competitions is a rite of passage for bartenders in Portland, as I can attest from personal experience.

Allison uses Highland Park 12 in this cocktail, which pairs very well with winter citrus and provides inspiration for the name via its distillery in the Orkney Islands of Scotland. Any good Scotch could work; just avoid particularly peaty ones, such as those associated with the Islay region.

The sweet vermouth called for in this drink is Carpano Antica, a distinctly flavorful brand. Typical vermouths are too mild to stand up to the other assertive ingredients in this drink, so it's worth picking up a bottle despite the higher price tag. It's very enjoyable outside of cocktails too, served on the rocks with an orange peel.

With Scotch, Carpano Antica, and oatmeal stout among the ingredients, this cocktail combines some very strong flavors. The egg white, citrus, and syrup smooth these out to strike a fine balance between sour, sweet, and bitter that drinks surprisingly easy.

IRON ISLAND

1 egg white

1 1/2 oz. Scotch

3/4 oz. fresh Meyer lemon juice

3/4 oz. Cider Syrup,
see recipe below

1/2 oz. Carpano Antica

1/2 oz. oatmeal stout

Combine the egg white, Scotch, lemon juice, syrup, and Carpano Antica in a cocktail shaker. Shake without ice to aerate the egg white, then add the oatmeal stout and ice. Shake again. Strain the drink into a cocktail glass.

Serves 1

CIDER SYRUP

1 cup (240 ml) apple cider

1/4 cup (60 ml) honey

2 sprigs fresh thyme

Combine the ingredients in a pot and simmer over medium heat until reduced by about half. Strain and store the syrup in a sealed bottle. It will keep in the refrigerator for about 2 weeks.

Makes about 3/4 cup (180 ml)

The Rickey originated at Shoomaker's bar in Washington, D.C., and was named after Democratic lobbyist Colonel Joe Rickey. The drink consisted of only a base spirit, the juice of half a lime, and mineral water—simple, but just right on one of D.C.'s notoriously humid summer days. Joe Rickey liked his with bourbon, but the version that caught on the most widely was made with gin. By 1925, the Gin Rickey was popular enough to merit an appearance in F. Scott Fitzgerald's *The Great Gatsby*. In 2011, the Washington city council proclaimed the Rickey to be the official drink of the District, and today the D.C. Craft Bartenders Guild celebrates Rickey Month every July.

In 2013, Tales of the Cocktail, the annual gathering of bartenders, spirits producers, and drink enthusiasts in New Orleans, hosted a competition to create a drink that would serve as the "official cocktail" of the conference. The challenge was to create a twist on the classic Rickey, updating the drink while keeping the original idea intact. Submissions had to use a base spirit, be tart with citrus, use little to no sweetener, have a bubbly element, and be served on the rocks in a tall glass or goblet. Having first learned to tend bar in Washington and realizing that beer could work as the carbonated ingredient, I couldn't resist entering a beer cocktail into the competition.

For the beer I chose a saison, which is my go-to in the summer months. Gin adds aromatics, a mere quarter ounce of Chartreuse

PORTLAND RICKEY

1 1/2 oz. gin

3/4 oz. fresh lemon juice

1/4 oz. Chartreuse (green)

4 oz. (120 ml) saison

Lemon shell, for garnish

Combine the ingredients in a highball glass over ice in the order listed, adding the beer last. Stir gently to combine. Save half a lemon squeezed for juice and drop it into the drink for garnish.

Serves 1

provides herbal complexity and a hint of sweetness, and a dose of lemon juice gives the drink bright acidity. A spent lime shell is the traditional garnish for a Rickey, so a lemon shell plays the same role here.

No one was surprised more than I when my submission ended up winning the competition and being served at the Tales of the Cocktail opening ceremony. To make it exactly as we did in New Orleans, use Martin Miller's gin and North Coast Le Merle Saison. However, any good gin and saison will do.

DETROITER

1 oz. Cynar

³/₄ oz. apple brandy

³/₄ oz. fresh lemon juice

³/₄ oz. Honey Syrup,
see recipe below

2 oz. (60 ml) IPA

Twist of grapefruit peel,
for garnish

Combine the Cynar, brandy, lemon juice, syrup, and 1 ounce of the IPA in a cocktail shaker. Shake without ice, then add ice and shake again. Strain the drink into an ice-filled rocks glass. Top with the remaining IPA and garnish with the grapefruit peel.

Serves 1

HONEY SYRUP

¹/₂ cup (120 ml) water

1 cup (240 ml) honey

In a pot, bring the water to a boil and add the honey, stirring until it is dissolved. Store the syrup in a sealed bottle at room temperature. It will keep for several weeks.

Makes 1 ¹/₄ cups (300 ml)

The Pacific Coast Highway is one of the most scenic drives in the United States, winding along the Pacific Ocean with spectacular cliffside views. Following its path south of Los Angeles also leads to one of my favorite places in the country to grab a drink, 320 Main in Seal Beach. That's where owner Jason Schiffer mixes up this deliciously bitter beer cocktail called the Detroiter.

Jason and I share a love for Michigan, he from growing up there and I from spending summers in the Upper Peninsula. He created this drink with a Michigan autumn in mind: "Apple cider, burning leaves, hay rides—all these sweet and earthy smells combine during the fall and I wanted to do my best to put that in a glass." The combination of apple brandy and bittersweet Cynar amaro pulls that off perfectly. Jason uses Stone IPA from San Diego in this cocktail since he now lives in Southern California, but those living closer to Michigan could choose an IPA from one of the more than one hundred breweries and brewpubs operating in the state.

Jason shakes this drink first without ice, then again with ice in the shaker. This "dry shake" helps froth up the beer to give the drink a soft head. An additional float of IPA after the drink is strained accentuates the beer's flavor even more.

SLOW CLAP

1 1/2 oz. Old Tom gin

3/4 oz. fresh lemon juice

1/2 oz. Chamomile Syrup,
see recipe below

1/2 oz. Cardamaro

3 oz. (90 ml) IPA

1 lemon wheel, for garnish

Combine the gin, lemon juice, syrup, and Cardamaro in a shaker and shake with ice. Strain into an ice-filled collins glass. Top with the IPA, stir lightly to integrate the beer, and garnish with the lemon wheel.

Serves 1

CHAMOMILE SYRUP

1 heaping tbsp. chamomile flowers

1 cup (240 ml) water just off the boil

Approximately 2 cups (400 g) sugar

Steep the chamomile in the water for 20 minutes, then strain out the chamomile. Measure the volume of remaining liquid and combine with twice the volume of sugar to make a rich syrup, heating if necessary to dissolve the sugar. Store refrigerated in a sealed, clean glass bottle. It will keep for several weeks.

Makes about 2 cups (480 ml)

In the 1800s, as bowls of punch gave way to cocktails, one of the classic drinks to emerge was the John Collins. It was essentially a gin punch in cocktail form: gin, lemon, sugar, and chilled soda water.

In making the crossing from England to the United States, its name somehow changed to Tom Collins. By the time Jerry Thomas released the 1876 edition of his *Bar-Tender's Guide*, Tom Collinses made with gin, whiskey, and brandy were common enough to merit inclusion.

The Collins is a prime candidate for adaptation as a beer cocktail, as this and the following recipe attest. They both employ a strong spirit, lemon juice, and a sweetening syrup as a foundation. Beer stands in for soda to extend the drink, making it light and refreshing. Splashes of aromatized wines are modern additions that bring a little more complexity.

The Slow Clap, from Ivy Mix of the Clover Club in New York, uses Old Tom gin as the base; Ivy suggests the barrel-aged Old Tom from Spring44 Distilling in Colorado. Cardamaro is an elegant wine-based aperitif flavored with cardoons, thistle, and other herbs. Chamomile tea syrup complements the floral notes of hops in an IPA; Clover Club uses Green Flash, but any aggressively hopped IPA could do well.

BEER BEAR-TAIL

1 oz. bourbon

1/2 oz. Cocchi Americano

1/2 oz. fresh lemon juice

1/4 oz. Rich Turbinado Syrup, *see recipe below*

3 to 4 oz. (90 to 120 ml) saison

Twist of orange peel, for garnish

Sprig of rosemary, for garnish

Combine the bourbon, Cocchi Americano, lemon juice, and syrup in a shaker and shake with ice. Strain into an ice-filled collins glass. Top with the saison, stir lightly to integrate the beer, and garnish with the orange peel and sprig of rosemary.

Serves 1

RICH TURBINADO SYRUP

1 cup (200 g) turbinado sugar

1/2 cup water

Combine the sugar and water in a pot. Heat and stir until the sugar is dissolved. Store refrigerated in a sealed, clean glass bottle. It will keep for several weeks.

Makes about 1 cup (240 ml)

Washington, D.C., has been famously described as a place of Southern efficiency and Northern charm. The city certainly took its time developing its drinking scene. In recent years, however, the nation's capital has come into its own as a drinking destination. I arrive on every visit with a long list of new local bars, beers, and spirits to try.

Usually at least one of these bars is owned by Derek Brown, whose establishments deserve much of the credit for elevating the District's cocktail culture. His newest, the wryly named Southern Efficiency whiskey bar, is the source of this cocktail, created by bartender J. P. Fetherston and his brother Éamonn.

This drink was created for one of the founders of 3 Stars Brewing Company, one of the new microbreweries to pop up in D.C. J. P. features 3 Stars' tasty peppercorn saison in the cocktail. It's a great choice if you're local; otherwise, substitute another good saison. The bourbon should be one with a high rye content and a lot of spice. J. P. suggests the Belle Meade bourbon, which has a rye-heavy mash bill and comes in at just over 90 proof.

Like the Slow Clap (opposite), this cocktail also uses aromatized wine to play up the floral and bitter notes in the drink. In this case it's Cocchi Americano, an aperitif flavored with cinchona, gentian, and other herbs and spices.

One of my taste testers declared the Beer Bear-Tail to be one of her favorite cocktails in the book. I'll definitely seek it out on my next visit.

WEISSECAR

1 ¼ oz. cognac

½ oz. Grand Marnier

½ oz. Simple Syrup, *see page 103*

½ oz. fresh lemon juice

1 ½ oz. hefeweizen

Lemon wedge, for garnish

Combine all the ingredients in a shaker and shake with ice. Strain the drink into a chilled cocktail glass. Garnish with the lemon wedge.

Serves 1

Brady Weise didn't name this cocktail after himself. The "weisse" in the name is a reference to the use of German wheat beer in the drink. Beer cocktails of all sorts are one of Brady's specialties, and his knowledge of beer dates back to taking up homebrewing when he was fifteen years old.

After bartending in Chicago, San Francisco, and now Los Angeles, he settled into his current home at 1886 Bar in Pasadena. There he oversees a menu known for its wildly creative cocktails and its frequent use of beer as an ingredient.

Of his beer cocktails that I've had the pleasure of trying, this variation on the Sidecar is my favorite. The classic Sidecar consists of just three ingredients, although getting the balance right among them can be a bit tricky.

Brady's addition of hefeweizen is inspired—there's that wheat beer and orange pairing again!—and takes the drink in a great direction. A touch of simple syrup rounds it out with a little sweetness.

Brady suggests a Bavarian hefeweizen for this drink; I've made it with Franziskaner, which is a classic and works very well.

DARK AND STOUTLY

1 1/2 oz. bourbon or
aged rum

1 1/2 oz. Ginger-Habanero Syrup,
see recipe below

3/4 oz. fresh lime juice

Stout or porter

Combine the bourbon, syrup,
and lime juice in a shaker and
shake them with ice. Strain the
drink into a pint glass filled
halfway with ice. Top it with
the stout, pouring gently to
achieve a layering effect. Mix
the drink with a spoon or straw,
if desired.

Serves 1

GINGER-HABANERO SYRUP

3 cups (600 g) turbinado sugar

1 pound (455 g) fresh ginger,
skin on, thinly sliced

1 habanero, halved and seeded
(use gloves!)

2 cups (480 ml) water

Combine the sugar, ginger,
habanero, and water in a pot and
heat over medium heat, stirring,
until the sugar has dissolved, then
bring it to a simmer. Remove the
pot from the heat and remove the
chile halves, or leave them in if
more spice is desired. Once cool,
strain the syrup and store it in a
sealed bottle. It will keep in the
refrigerator for up to 2 weeks.

Makes about 4 cups (960 ml)

I met Chicago-based mixologist Adam Seger in 2008 when he tended bar at Nacional 27, where I'd sought him out to try a cigar-infused Manhattan he'd put on the menu. Since then he's gone on to produce his own botanical spirit called Hum, write menus for iPic movie theaters across the United States and the W Hotel in Singapore, and create the welcome cocktail for the 84th Academy Awards Governors Ball, among other honors. He also has a cocktail book of his own in the works.

I met Adam again a few years later during San Antonio Cocktail Week when he was doing a guest bartending shift devoted to beer cocktails, which had become a passion of his as well. He created this one as a variation on the Dark and Stormy cocktail, pairing dark rum or bourbon with a spicy ginger-habanero syrup.

It's not as hot as it sounds, with the ginger contributing more heat than the pepper. Nonetheless, he suggests a nitrogen cask beer with a creamy head to help tame the habanero.

Two of his favorite stouts for this beer are Boulevard Dry Stout and Monk's Stout from Dupont. He serves it layered, which is a striking presentation. However, when it comes to drinking it, I like to mix it all together.

BOLT CUTTER

1 1/2 oz. cream sherry

1 oz. Russian Imperial Stout Orgeat, *see recipe below*

3/4 oz. fresh lime juice

3/4 oz. fresh grapefruit juice

1/2 oz. Smith & Cross rum

1/2 oz. Wray & Nephew overproof white rum

Lime wedge, for garnish

Sprig of fresh mint, for garnish

Combine the cream sherry, orgeat, citrus juices, and rums in a shaker and shake with ice. Strain the drink into a rocks glass filled with crushed ice. Garnish with the lime wedge and sprig of mint.

Serves 1

RUSSIAN IMPERIAL STOUT ORGEAT

12 oz. (360 ml) Russian imperial stout

1 cup (150 g) blanched chopped almonds

About 1 1/2 cups (300 g) sugar

1/8 tsp. orange flower water

In a pot, heat the imperial stout and almonds over medium heat to about 150°F (65°C). Let them stand for about 5 minutes, then transfer the mixture to a blender and pulse. Let it stand for 15 minutes. Repeat this process three more times. Strain the liquid through a fine-mesh strainer, discard the solids, and measure the volume of the resulting almond milk. Put it in a pot and add one and a half times that amount of sugar (i.e., use 1 1/2 cups sugar for 1 cup liquid). Heat and stir until the sugar has dissolved, then add the orange flower water. Store the orgeat in a sealed glass bottle in the refrigerator. It will keep for several weeks.

Makes about 1 1/2 cups (360 ml)

Several of the recipes in this book call for orgeat, a flavorful almond syrup used in tiki cocktails. While there are good commercial brands available, Niklas Morris of the Tough Luck Club in Tucson, Arizona, gets creative with a housemade version using Russian imperial stout. The process blends the nutty sweetness of orgeat with the roasty notes of a rich stout.

This cocktail is an unexpected combination of ingredients that works exceptionally well. It goes down so smoothly, rounded out by orgeat and cream sherry, that you might never guess it's made with two very high-proof rums. Specific brands are recommended in the recipe, as the drink benefits from these distinctively aromatic Jamaican rums. Sip with restraint and enjoy.

Bolt Cutter is a phrase Niklas's grandfather uses to describe an especially strong wind. With imperial stout and two high-proof rums, it's an apt name.

Although immensely popular, vodka appears rarely in the canon of classic cocktails. And like many contemporary bartenders, I don't often reach for a bottle when I'm working on new drinks. Vodka is legally defined in the United States as being "without distinctive character, aroma, taste, or color." When there are ingredients on hand like gin, whiskey, or rum, which offer so much complexity, making a vodka cocktail can seem unexciting.

I was especially skeptical of using vodka in a beer cocktail until Brady Weise won me over with this drink at his bar at the Raymond in Pasadena, California. As the name suggests, it's inspired by the White Russian, also known as a "Caucasian" to the titular character in *The Big Lebowski*. Like the Dude himself, I've been known to indulge in a few White Russians from time to time, though I do try to be dressed and out of my bathrobe first.

Instead of calling for a coffee liqueur, this drink gets its roasty notes from crème de cacao and rich stout. For the former, I recommend the luscious crème de cacao from Tempus Fugit Spirits, which is a revelation if one has only tried the typical versions of the liqueur. With a full ounce of crème de cacao being used here, it's worth picking up a good one.

There are many stouts that could do well here; Brady and I both like the Yeti Imperial Stout from Great Divide in Denver. Brady also suggests trying a coffee stout, such as Modern Times Black House from San Diego. A float of lightly whipped cream provides the finishing touch. Don't omit it; it really ties the drink together.

LEBOWSKI ACHIEVER

1 1/2 oz. vodka

1 oz. crème de cacao

4 oz. (120 ml) heavy stout

1 oz. heavy cream, lightly whipped

Add the vodka and crème de cacao to a mixing glass and stir briefly with ice. Strain into an ice-filled collins glass. Top with the stout, then float the lightly whipped cream on top.

Serves 1

"Because Last Word variations jumped the shark like six years ago . . ." That was the knowing way Allan Katz and Danielle Crouch introduced this drink on their menu at Caña Rum Bar in downtown Los Angeles, one of my favorite bars in the country in which to relax with a glass of rum, a good cigar, and the occasional beer cocktail.

The Last Word—an equal-parts mix of gin, lime juice, maraschino liqueur, and Chartreuse dating back to Prohibition—is one of those classic cocktails that lends itself to infinite variation. Change one of the ingredients and voilà! A new cocktail is born. Many mixologists, this author among them, have used that formula as a crutch to creativity.

Does the world need yet another variation on the Last Word? If it's Caña's Curse Word, then the answer is yes. This version switches out the Chartreuse for Bitter Truth EXR, a German herbal liqueur that packs a more bitter punch than Chartreuse. The real genius of the drink is the addition of Belgian pale ale, which provides even more complexity and a hint of carbonation. This is a strong drink that goes down very easily.

To make it just like they do at Caña, use Tanqueray for the gin, Maraska for the maraschino, and La Chouffe Blonde for the beer.

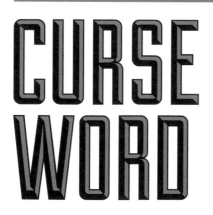

CURSE WORD

3/4 oz. gin

3/4 oz. Bitter Truth EXR

3/4 oz. maraschino liqueur

3/4 oz. fresh lime juice

1 oz. Belgian pale ale

Combine the gin, EXR, maraschino liqueur, and lime juice in a shaker and shake with ice. Strain the drink into a chilled cocktail glass. Top it with the pale ale, stirring gently to incorporate.

Serves 1

BLANKET FINISH

1 1/2 oz. Byrrh

1/2 oz. fresh
lemon juice

1/2 oz.
Benedictine

2 dashes
orange bitters

3 to 4 oz.
(90 to 120 ml)
IPA

Twist of
lemon peel,
for garnish

Combine the Byrrh, lemon juice,
Benedictine, and bitters in a
cocktail glass with several large
ice cubes. Stir briefly, then add
the IPA. Stir again to mix
and garnish with the lemon peel.

Serves 1

This cocktail could get confusing. It's a beer cocktail made with Byrrh, a French aperitif that is also pronounced "beer." Ordering Byrrh in a bar can be difficult for that reason. This is a Byrrh-beer cocktail; it has Byrrh and beer in it. Describing the recipe is, thankfully, easier to do in print than verbally.

Byrrh is a *quinquina*, an aperitif flavored with quinine, the cinchona bark extract that gives tonic water its distinct flavor. Wine-based *quinquinas* were developed in France in the mid-1800s to treat malaria; the wine and other herbs helped the medicinal quinine go down. Dubonnet and Lillet are the two most recognizable brands on the American market. Byrrh is a recent reintroduction here, though it appears occasionally in vintage cocktail books. Made from a blend of *mistelle*—grape must that has had its fermentation halted by

the addition of alcohol—and dry red wine, it has a sweet fruitiness that nicely complements the bitterness of quinine.

It's this quinine flavor that appeals to Ansel Vickery, the bar manager at the great neighborhood bar Free House in Portland, Oregon. Ansel aimed to make a cross between a Gin and Tonic and a Shandy. It has a little herbal sweetness from Benedictine, a balancing acidity from lemon, and a strong bitter backbone from Byrrh, IPA, and orange bitters. It all comes together in a perfectly balanced cocktail.

The Free House bartenders get inspiration from horse racing lingo for naming many of their cocktails. A "blanket finish" refers to a race ending so close that a blanket could cover the contestants.

AVERNA STOUT FLIP

1 large egg

2 oz. (60 ml) Averna

1 oz. stout

2 dashes Angostura bitters

Freshly grated nutmeg, for garnish

Crack the egg into a shaker, then add the Averna, stout, and bitters. Add ice and shake hard. Strain the drink into a wine or cocktail glass and garnish with freshly grated nutmeg.

Serves 1

Sometimes perfecting a cocktail recipe requires endless tinkering and many failed attempts dumped unceremoniously down the drain. At other, happier times, everything magically comes together on the first try. Such was the case with the Averna Stout Flip, which I created on the spur of the moment during a guest bartending stint at Portland's Prohibition-themed cocktail bar Circa 33 for a friend who asked me to surprise her. I've made it many times since, and it's become my favorite of the beer cocktails I've created.

Combining dark beer and dark spirits is a great formula for coming up with novel takes on the Flip. Carbonation from beer helps lighten the drink, while dark malts provide bitter, roasty flavors. In this one, stout pairs with the bittersweet liqueur Averna, a classic Italian amaro produced in Sicily.

When making this cocktail, reach for a big, heavy stout. Two of my favorite brews for this drink are Young's Double Chocolate Stout and Samuel Smith's Oatmeal Stout, but any rich dark beer will do.

The slightly syrupy Averna combines with the egg and stout to make a rich, dessertlike cocktail; think of it as a boozy milkshake. When I host beer cocktail events, this is often the drink I recommend to end the night. And with that in mind, it's also the drink with which I end this book.

BOOKS AND WEBSITES

Very few contemporary books exist on the topic of beer cocktails. The ones below are useful references, some for the recipes they contain and others for the colorful historic context they provide.

Abbott, Edward. *English and Australian Cookery Book.* London: Sampson Low, Son, and Marston, 1864.

Acitelli, Tom. *The Audacity of Hops.* Chicago: Chicago Review Press, 2013.

Baker, Charles H., Jr. *Jigger, Beaker, and Glass.* New York: Derrydale Press, 1992.

Berry, Jeff. *Sippin' Safari.* San Jose: Club Tiki Press, 2007.

Brown, John Hull. *Early American Beverages.* New York: Bonanza Books, 1966.

Cook, Richard. *Oxford Night Caps.* Chicago: Kalevala Books, 1871.

Curtis, Wayne. *And a Bottle of Rum.* New York: Three Rivers Press, 2006.

Dickens, Cedric. *Drinking with Dickens.* New York: New Amsterdam Books, 1980.

Doxat, John. *Booth's Handbook of Cocktails and Mixed Drinks.* London: Pan Books, 1966.

Earle, Alice Morse. *Customs and Fashions of Old New England.* New York: Charles Scribner's Sons, 1893.

Editors of Esquire. *Esquire's Handbook for Hosts.* New York: Grosset and Dunlap, 1949.

Hartley, Dorothy. *Food in England.* London: Macdonald, 1954.

Kappeler, George J. *Modern American Drinks.* New York: Merriam, 1895.

Marchant, W. T. *In Praise of Ale.* London: George Redway, 1888.

Ogle, Maureen. *Ambitious Brew.* New York: Harcourt, 2006.

Oliver, Garrett. *The Brewmaster's Table.* New York: Harper Collins, 2003.

Philp, Robert Kemp. *The Practical Housewife.* London: Houlston and Wright, 1860.

Schmidt, William. *The Flowing Bowl.* New York: Charles L. Webster, 1892.

Solmonson, David, and Lesley Jacobs Solmonson. *The 12 Bottle Bar.* New York: Workman, 2014.

Solmonson, Lesley Jacobs. *Gin.* London: Reaktion Books, 2012.

Spencer, Edward. *Cakes and Ale.* London: Stanley Paul, 1897.

Stelzer, Howard, and Ashley Stelzer. *Beer Cocktails.* Boston: Harvard Common Press, 2012.

Terrington, William. *Cooling Cups and Dainty Drinks.* New York: George Routledge and Sons, 1869.

Thomas, Jerry. *How to Mix Drinks.* New York: Dick and Fitzgerald, 1862.

Webb, Tim, and Stephen Beaumont. *The World Atlas of Beer.* New York: Sterling Epicure, 2012.

Wondrich, David. *Imbibe!* New York: Penguin, 2007.

——. *Punch.* New York: Penguin, 2010.

There are more websites and blogs dedicated to beer, spirits, and cocktails than anyone can possibly keep up with. The following are ones I follow and find consistently worth reading.

12 Bottle Bar, David Solmonson and Lesley Jacobs Solmonson, *www.12bottlebar.com*

Art of Drink, Darcy O'Neil, *www.artofdrink.com*

Beeronomics, Patrick Emerson, *www.beeronomics.blogspot.com*

Beervana, Jeff Alworth, *www.beervana.blogspot.com*

Brewpublic, Angelo de Ieso, *www.brewpublic.com*

The Chuck Cowdery Blog, Chuck Cowdery, *www.chuckcowdery.blogspot.com*

The Cocktail Chronicles, Paul Clarke, *www.cocktailchronicles.com*

A Dash of Bitters, Michael Dietsch, *www.adashofbitters.com*

Imbibe Unfiltered, *www.imbibemagazine .blogspot.com*

Jeffrey Morgenthaler, *www.jeffreymorgenthaler.com*

The New School, Ezra Johnson-Greenough, *www.newschoolbeer.com*

Observation Post, Maureen Ogle, *www.maureenogle.com*

The Pegu Blog, Doug Winship, *www.killingtime.com/Pegu*

Professor Cocktail, David J. Montgomery, *www.professorcocktail.com*

Punch, *www.punchdrink.com*

RumDood, Matt Robold, *www.rumdood.com*

The Weissecar (page 139)

SELECTED BARS

Keeping track of which bars serve beer cocktails can be a challenge. Bars come and go, and menus and staff change all the time. That said, the following are some promising possibilities.

ARIZONA
Tough Luck Club, Tucson

CALIFORNIA
1886 Bar, Pasadena
320 Main, Seal Beach
Alembic, San Francisco
Bestia, Los Angeles
Big Bar, Los Angeles
Caña, Los Angeles
Craft & Commerce, San Diego
The Last Word, Livermore
Library Bar, Los Angeles
LowBrau, Sacramento
Polite Provisions, San Diego
Sassafras Saloon, Los Angeles

COLORADO
Bōl, Vail
Euclid Hall, Denver
Star Bar, Denver
Ste. Ellie, Denver

DISTRICT OF COLUMBIA
Baby Wale, D.C.
Belga Café, D.C.
Pizzeria Paradiso, D.C.
Queen Vic, D.C.
Rogue 24, D.C.
Southern Efficiency, D.C.

GEORGIA
Paper Plane, Decatur
Sprig, Decatur

ILLINOIS
Analogue, Chicago
The Gage, Chicago

LOUISIANA
Twelve Mile Limit, New Orleans
Loa, New Orleans

MASSACHUSETTS
Russell House Tavern, Cambridge
Trina's Starlite Lounge, Somerville

NEW YORK
Betony, New York
The Breslin, New York
Clover Club, New York
The Dead Rabbit, New York
Mayahuel, New York
PDT, New York
Rosa Mexicano, New York
Saxon + Parole, New York

OREGON
Bazi Bierbasserie, Portland
Clyde Common, Portland
Free House, Portland
The Hop and Vine, Portland
Teardrop Cocktail Lounge, Portland

PENNSYLVANIA
The Dandelion Pub, Philadelphia

TENNESSEE
Holland House Bar and Refuge, Nashville

TEXAS
Anvil Bar and Refuge, Houston
Bar Congress, Austin
The Brew Exchange, Austin

VIRGINIA
Virtue Feed & Grain, Alexandria

WASHINGTON
Barrio, Seatte
Canon, Seattle
Rob Roy, Seattle

GLOBAL
BrewDog Craft Beer Bars, multiple locations, UK
Josephine's, Antwerp, BE
Purl, London, UK

RESOURCES

The online stores listed below are good sources for some of the equipment and ingredients used in this book.

BarProducts.com
www.barproducts.com

The Boston Shaker
www.thebostonshaker.com

Cocktail Kingdom
www.cocktailkingdom.com

Crate & Barrel
www.crateandbarrel.com

The Dead Rabbit
www.deadrabbitnyc.com

F. H. Steinbart
www.fhsteinbart.com

GermanDeli.com
www.germandeli.com

The Meadow
www.atthemeadow.com

PolyScience
www.polyscience.com

Sur La Table
www.surlatable.com

Williams-Sonoma
www.williams-sonoma.com

ACKNOWLEDGMENTS

BRINGING ONE'S FIRST BOOK INTO THE WORLD IS A DAUNTING EXPERIENCE. GETTING *COCKTAILS ON TAP* INTO PRINT REQUIRED THREE YEARS OF EFFORT.

I couldn't have done it without the invaluable guidance from cookbook author Diane Morgan, who advised me early on about how to write a compelling proposal, find an agent, and pitch to editors. Early attempts to get the book into print also benefited from advice and assistance from Ellee Thalheimer, Lucy Burningham, Maureen Ogle, Stephen Beaumont, Evan Rail, Ryan French, Ben Mercer, and Ritch Marvin.

The recipes included here have benefited from extensive taste tests from many friends who put up with the occasional strange brew in exchange for free beer and liquor. Their feedback and patience were invaluable, especially in their willingness to try out some of the weirder drinks dug up in the course of my cocktail archeology. Amy Wolfenberger, Tom Samson, Kristen McGillivray, Paul and Michelle Willenberg, Tim Brandis, Trina Siebert, Havilah Howard, Matt Helsey, Jussi Heikkola, Denise Johnson, Ben Edmunds, Ron Dollete, John the Bastard, Nathan Zilka, Anthony Cafiero, Juliana Young, and Kyle Linden Webster all contributed their palates to the refinement of the recipes. Testing these took me everywhere from a blacksmith's shop to a modernist kitchen.

The idea for a book of beer cocktails would have never come to fruition without the creative impulse of beer writer and event organizer Ezra Johnson-Greenough, who invited bar owner Yetta Vorobik and me to create the Brewing Up Cocktails series of events focused on using beer as an ingredient. A number of spirits brands and breweries lent their support to these events, including Bols Genever, El Dorado Rum, Drambuie, Novo Fogo Cachaça, Tempus Fugit Spirits, Combier, Kona Brewing, Ninkasi Brewing, and Oakshire Brewing.

I owe my bartending career to a few people who were willing to take a chance on a cocktail blogger with limited experience, especially Lance Mayhew, Neil Kopplin, and Bruce Goldberg. Todd Steele of Metrovino brought me back into the fold when I thought my bartending days were behind me, tolerated my travel schedule, and supported me putting beer cocktails on the menu despite the fact that we were mostly a wine bar.

I'm extremely grateful to the bartenders who contributed recipes

for consideration in the book. Their creativity made my job a heck of a lot easier. I could have tried to fill the book with dozens of my own recipes, but trust me, it's better this way.

The proposal for this book was dead in the water until my agent, Jud Laghi, picked it up. The book wouldn't exist without him, and for that he deserves more than his standard cut of the royalties (but don't tell him that). Laura Dozier, my editor at Stewart, Tabori & Chang, has been a pleasure to work with; her suggestions for improvement have always been spot on, and I'm thankful she had the vision to bring this unusual idea for a book into print.

I am thrilled beyond words that David L. Reamer agreed to shoot the book and jumped into the project with such enthusiasm. I approached him with the idea mostly as a formality, almost certain he'd be tied up shooting for some James Beard Award-winning chef. His eye for food and drink and his persistence in finding the perfect shot make him one of the best in the business. Regardless of how the drinks tasted, I knew that with him behind the camera, they would at least look good. (Don't worry, they taste good too.)

Getting out of the studio and into some of Portland's most scenic bars and restaurants allowed us to get some great drink shots. My thanks to Raven & Rose, Ración, Ned Ludd, the Richmond, and the "Irvington Bierstube" for letting us invade their spaces. The Albina Press, Red E Café, and Ristretto Roasters are some of the nicest coffee shops a freelance writer could ask for, keeping me focused and my laptop battery charged.

Finally, this book owes a great deal to Portland's unique culture of collaboration, obsession with quality food and drink, and amazing beer and cocktail communities. It's hard to imagine this project coming together in quite the same way anywhere else.

INDEX

Page numbers in *italics* refer to photographs.

BEER + CLASSIC COCKTAIL INDEX

Give the beer-enhanced version of your favorite classic drink a shot! Pun intended. It might be more complex, interesting, satisfying, and just plain better than the original.

Published in 2015 by Stewart, Tabori & Chang
An imprint of ABRAMS

Text copyright © 2015 by Jacob Grier
Photographs copyright © 2015 by
David L. Reamer
Foreword copyright © 2015 by
Stephen Beaumont

Library of Congress Control Number:
2014942970

ISBN: 978-1-61769-142-3

Editor: Laura Dozier
Designer: Strick&Williams
Illustrator: Ariana Nehmad Ross
Production Manager: Denise LaCongo

The text of this book was composed in
Duke and Vitesse.

Printed and bound in the United States

10 9 8 7 6 5 4 3 2 1

Stewart, Tabori & Chang books are available at
special discounts when purchased in quantity
for premiums and promotions as well as fund-
raising or educational use. Special editions
can also be created to specification. For details,
contact specialsales@abramsbooks.com or the
address below.

ABRAMS
THE ART OF BOOKS SINCE 1949

115 West 18th Street
New York, NY 10011
www.abramsbooks.com